Henry L Jephson

Notes on Irish questions

Henry L Jephson
Notes on Irish questions
ISBN/EAN: 9783744740807
Printed in Europe, USA, Canada, Australia, Japan
Cover: Foto ©ninafisch / pixelio.de

More available books at **www.hansebooks.com**

SIDELIGHTS ON THE
HOME RULE MOVEMENT

First Edition . . . *May,* 1906.
Reprinted . . . . . *June,* 1906.

NOTES ON IRISH QUESTIONS.

DUBLIN:
PRINTED BY PORTEOUS AND GIBBS,
18 Wicklow Street.

NOTES

ON

IRISH QUESTIONS.

BY

HENRY L. JEPHSON.

BOSTON COLLEGE LIBRARY
CHESTNUT HILL, MASS.

DUBLIN:
WILLIAM McGEE, 18 NASSAU STREET.
LONDON:
LONGMANS, GREEN, AND CO.
1870.

PREFACE.

It is but fair to whoever may be inclined to consult the following pages, to state the object which the writer had in view in compiling them, and in laying them before the public.

The reader will thus, in some degree, be apprized beforehand as to whether he is likely or not to find in them the kind of information he may be in search of, in regard to the subjects usually included under the denomination of "Irish Questions."

It has been the lot of the writer (and whose has it not been?) to be present at innumerable discussions upon the political and social condition of Ireland. Its unmerited wrongs, according to some; its inevitable misfortunes, according to others; or a combination of these, have been passed in review; their supposed causes assigned, and imagined remedies for them proposed. On such occasions, the warmth of party spirit has sometimes prevailed, sometimes the earnestness of true patriotism, with strange dissonance of feeling and opinion, it is true, but with a melancholy unanimity as to one disheartening fact—namely, that Ireland, this vital portion of the British empire, this essential element of its existence in Europe as a first-rate power, has been, and continues to be, an exception to the well-being of the other members of the body to which it belongs; and instead of being one of the pillars of its greatness, forms the very weakest part of the fabric.

There are, unfortunately, those who rejoice that this is so; there are those who deplore it; but all agree as to the fact.

Neither the experience of the author nor such information as he had been able to acquire, qualified him to be more than an humble, though highly interested, listener at such debates. With this, he could have been contented, had he found that in such a capacity his comprehension of the various questions discussed grew clearer, or his knowledge of the occurrences connected with them increased. But he was conscious that such was not the case. What forced itself upon his attention was, that speakers, as well as writers, on this subject, were not only out of all unison with each other in sentiment and opinion, but continually at variance as to *facts*. It was this consideration which begat in him a desire to set down in order, for his own use, and to digest into the form of short notes, an account of the principal legislative and administrative measures which have been applied by the Imperial Government of Great Britain as cures or palliatives of the admitted evils under which this country has been labouring. It was his desire to state, as far as it could be distinctly done, the motives with which these various enactments had been framed; the prevailing political or economical doctrines, in conformity with which they were meant to be applied; and in so far as tangible results can now be obtained, to mark their success or failure, whether entire or partial, in furthering the particular objects which they were intended to effect.

It will be seen that this plan leaves little room for what are usually termed "appreciations." The author has no pretension to present his readers with discoveries or disclosures. He purposely abstains from any attempt to award praise or blame to persons or parties engaged in the affairs of Ireland, and still less does he presume to offer any "panacea" of his own invention for their settlement. This, it is true, reduces the scope of his work to what may by many be considered to be very humble proportions; but there are nevertheless circumstances connected with the cotemporary history of public events and legislative measures, which may render such a recapitulation and abstract of them, as is now attempted, of use to many. With regard to such occurrences and measures the public lives, so to say, from day to day. Events or measures are canvassed with eagerness and examined with minuteness, at the time they come immediately under public discussion; but they are soon set aside or forgotten, to make room for matters more exciting or more pressing; and at all events their connection one with another, as links in a chain of policy, or necessary steps in the sequence of political events, is almost always lost sight of.

It may be said that the subject is trite, and the documents relating to it public and accessible. But in this instance the materials are very multifarious in kind and voluminous in bulk. The evidence respecting the state of Ireland is dispersed amongst the Reports of Parliamentary Proceedings and occasional works, not easily met with except in large libraries.

Committees were appointed at different times to inquire into subjects regarding the state of Ireland and the evidence there taken is of the greatest importance to a right understanding of the questions involved. The gentlemen examined before these committees represented every shade of opinion, Protestant or Roman Catholic, landlord or tenant, employer or labourer, and they were persons possessing minute local knowledge of the country, while they included in their number both statesmen and economists. Evidence of the most reliable and authentic description has been produced; but it often lies hid under a mass of less interesting matter, and cannot be brought to bear upon the present state of things without selection.

The author is not aware that any similar attempt has been made; and his position happened to be one which afforded him a somewhat readier access to the materials in question than is usually enjoyed by the general public. A feeling that his labour had not been altogether unprofitable to himself, led him to believe that it might be useful to others, and this alone is his motive for the present publication.

TABLE OF CONTENTS.

Chap.	Page.
I.—Introductory Chapter	1
II.—Ireland in 1825	16
III.—Condition of the Lower Classes in 1825	34
IV.—The Sub-Letting Act	50
V.—Administration of Justice	68
VI.—Crime	102
VII.—Roman Catholic Emancipation	132
VIII.—The Forty-shilling Freeholders	147
IX.—Tithes and Church Rates	162
X.—National Education	179
XI.—Public Works	199
XII.—Poor Law	215
XIII.—Municipal Corporations	246
XIV.—The Famine	257
XV.—Incumbered Estates Act	278
XVI.—Emigration	290
XVII.—Agriculture—Land Improvement Act, &c.	309
XVIII.—Material Progress of Ireland	324
Conclusion	334

CHAPTER I.

INTRODUCTORY—REVIEW OF IRISH HISTORY to 1826, AND REASONS FOR ENTERING UPON A MORE DETAILED INVESTIGATION OF IT FROM THAT YEAR.

THE author of the following notes has chosen to date them from the year 1826, because it appeared to him that it was then that the attention of the British Government was for the first time seriously directed to the problem of governing Ireland, not as a dependency, but as an integral part of the empire.

It was about this time, too, that a blind faith in the truth of certain erroneous commercial and economical dogmas, which, in common with the rest of the world, had long subsisted in England with all the authority of fundamental articles of belief, began to be questioned.

The result had been that many of these doctrines, if not yet altogether discredited, had nevertheless been considerably modified ; and important enactments had already been made in consonance with those sounder principles which have since prevailed.

When we have shown, as we hope to be able to do, that it was the rigorous application of these accepted, but mischievous, economic maxims to the affairs of Ireland, that, more than perhaps any other circumstance, retarded her progress, and everywhere injurious, from peculiar circumstances in her case, proved absolutely destructive to every germ of prosperity and consequent civilization, it will more easily be understood why the year 1826 has been selected as a period at which the dawn of a better day for Ireland had at length made itself visible.

In fixing upon this, or any other particular epoch, as a starting point for such an investigation, it is far from the intention of the author to undervalue, and much less to dispense with, the necessity of a conscientious study of the previous history of Ireland, so far as it can be correctly ascertained. Obscure and confused as this history may appear to many, a knowledge of it is essential to a proper understanding of the real position of things even at the present day. It usually proves uninteresting to the general reader, not from a want of incidents sufficiently stirring to awake attention, but from the monotony attending an eternal repetition of the same scenes of violence and misery, while the materials of Irish story were never, as Sallust remarks in regard to the annals of the Athenians, raised from insignificance or dulness by the genius of their historians.

They present all the terrible phases of a prolonged struggle between a semi-civilized conqueror and an almost barbarous and but half-subdued vassal : iron-handed, but ill-organized, tyranny and corruption on the one side, contending with the ferocious and treacherous retaliation of the savage on the other. The very inefficiency of the early English rule in Ireland seems to have rendered it doubly oppressive. Rebellion succeeded rebellion, never quite successful, but never thoroughly quelled, though often relentlessly revenged—never prevented by the wisdom of rulers, or, to use a now much hackneyed expression, "stamped out" by their resolution and firmness.

Such was the history of Ireland for ages—perhaps for a longer period than that of any other European country ; and it was from the state of things resulting from these events that she had to emerge and take her place among the civilised nations of the world.

By what seems an accumulation of ill fortune, the day of peace and of possible improvement was in her case still further postponed, when in other countries it seemed to have arrived, in consequence of the termination in one way or another, of the great religious contest which had convulsed Europe for a century and a-half.

In this contest, Ireland, like the rest, had been obliged to play her part; all the miseries and the bitterness of the struggle had been hers—its very last battle had, in fact, been fought upon her soil—but without giving to her even the melancholy advantage, resulting to every other country where the controversy raged, of a final settlement of the dispute. Deplorable as had been the means by which this had in most cases been effected, the fruit was so far good, that further dissension was comparatively at an end. France, by the extermination and banishment of her Protestant subjects had at length become undividedly Catholic. Spain, by analogous means, had kept or re-established the Roman Catholic faith both at home and in what remained to her of her Flemish dominion. Catholicism had been retained or reconstituted in part of Germany, while a distinct portion of that country, together with Holland, Denmark, Sweden, and, lastly, England and Scotland, had become the undisputed seats of Protestant communities. But it was the singular ill-fortune of Ireland, that in her case neither of these solutions were in reality arrived at. The Protestant religion was, it is true, ultimately established as that of the British empire—with respect to England and Scotland *really*—with respect to Ireland *apparently* only. A Protestant minority, supported by or recruited from the ranks of their co-religionists in Great Britain, had subdued the rest and constrained them to a nominal acquiescence with the faith of their conquerors; but whether from the ignorance resulting from their barbarous condition, or, as is more probable, from a blind hatred of the religion of those whom they had traditionally regarded as their oppressors, a vast majority of the Irish, properly so-called, remained passionately attached to the only religious faith with which they had any acquaintance, and to one which, whatever we may think of it, we cannot but admit to have something in it more congenial to their natural disposition, temperament, and condition, than the purer form adopted by the superior reason and enlightenment of their English and Scotch fellow-subjects.

To rectify this inequality in the numbers of those who in Ireland represented the established Government of Britain, and of those who it was obvious must continue to be vehemently opposed to it, and who would consequently never omit an opportunity of overturning it, it became necessary to adopt, so to say, one of those systematic measures of State absolutely required on the part of the English, if Ireland was to be governed by them at all, either as a part or a dependency of the empire.

Had the Government of England been a pure despotism, where the will of the sovereign is exercised directly and indiscriminately by the engines of a central administration on its friends and foes without any delegation of its privileges to the one or to the other, the problem of governing a country so situated as Ireland would still have been difficult, and the process rude and cruel; but at least the object of maintaining authority might have been attained, while the enduring animosity between class and class, religion and religion, race and race, a thousand times more terrible and more destructive to the happiness and prosperity of a nation than the most absolute personal tyranny that ever yet subsisted, might have been forgotten.

But it must be recollected that the genius of the English Government itself partook, even at that time, of what is now termed "self-government." Less so than at present, no doubt, but still it had never undergone the process of "centralization," which had taken place in almost every other European country. The people, however high the prerogative of the Crown, practically administered the laws upon themselves, collected or represented in assemblies of various denominations; and the local government of each province or county supplied the daily requirements of government and police, without the intervention of the supreme authority of the State.

Such a polity is in general not only conducive to liberty, but may be considered in a great measure to constitute it. At all events, the idea that institutions of this kind were the necessary constituents of Government and the inherited right of the people, had become inherent in the Anglo-Saxon race which predominated in Great Britain; and in extending the rule of England over the uncivilized tribes who inhabited rather than governed Ireland, it never occurred to the conquerors that this was to be done through the medium of any other forms than those under which they themselves had hitherto lived.

It became, however, immediately evident, that the application of institutions which had grown up in England, under one set of circumstances, could not, without essential modifications, be transplanted to Ireland, where an entirely different state of things had ever prevailed.

The fundamental difference consisted in this — that what in England served to secure the liberty of a people who all acknowledged the authority of a common government, had in Ireland to be used for the purpose of subjugating one part of the population by the other. When by far the greater portion of it had either never acknowledged, or was ever ready to throw off, its allegiance to the sovereign, it was clearly impossible to extend to it rights or privileges which would have been immediately used for the overthrow of his authority.

In preserving, therefore, in any degree the forms of municipal self-government, it became absolutely necessary that its exercise should be confined to those whose loyalty to the Crown of England could be depended upon; in other words, either to those of purely English origin who had subdued or colonized the country, or to those few of the natives who had joined their ranks. It is sufficiently obvious, that from this principle a state of things must have resulted productive of the most galling and most humiliating of all the forms of oppression to which a nation can be liable from its governors. Where, as in the case of Ireland, the conquest of the whole country had never been complete, the evils of this kind of government are infinitely increased, and the mutual animosities of the parties are indefinitely prolonged. To such a country even the peace which follows the submission of despair is denied; imagined rights are never forgotten by the conquered, and when manifested in acts of resistance must be crushed by fresh measures of coercion by the conquerors. When these constitute but a minority, it is evident that such measures are the more readily adopted, from their having all the necessities of acts of self-defence. If what were called the " mere Irish " were in their rebellion fighting for what they deemed their native rights, the English conquerors, or colonists, were fighting for their lives, as well as for their newly acquired properties. Defeat would to them have implied extermination; and, it is needless to observe, that men in such circumstances are seldom restrained by considerations of morality or humanity, in regard to the means which they use for the maintenance of their rule.

Such was, in fact, the position of the English settlers in Ireland. The aid they received from their own Government was generally fitful and inefficient, irregularly afforded and inopportunely withdrawn, according to circumstances more immediately affecting the central parts of the empire. These "puttings down of rebellion" in Ireland partook more the character of chastisement, or passing revenge, than that of a steady resolution to establish a permanent authority. Ireland was, in fact, in those times looked upon as a country barbarous and remote, inferior in all respects to England, a field of desperate adventure, not intended or destined ever to become either a sister kingdom, or an integral part of that of Britain; but to use the word of the Statute, (6 Geo. I., cap. 5,) one "that is and ought to be *subordinate* to, and *dependent upon*, the Imperial Crown of Great Britain, as being inseparably united thereto."*

The idea of the inherent inferiority of Ireland was, in fact, long maintained, although it, no doubt, became gradually softened; and it was accompanied by a jealousy of even its material or commercial prosperity, founded upon this feeling as well as upon those false principles of commercial

---

* See "Blackstone's Commentaries," Kerr's Edition, vol. i., pp. 85 and 86.

economy to which we have alluded, in virtue of which the prosperity of a nation was believed to depend, not so much on its own absolute riches or productive power, as from the comparative poverty and unproductiveness of its neighbours.

This erroneous doctrine was not only applied to the case of foreign nations, but to that of each of the provinces of the same nation. Did any particular county produce better cattle or better crops of any sort than elsewhere, it was considered sound commercial policy to prevent or discourage by every possible means similar productions in any other part of the kingdom. Can we then feel surprise, that when it was found that Ireland was able to supply the English markets at a cheap rate with one of the prime necessaries of life, its importation was met not only with high duties, but by actual prohibition, and that it was solemnly proposed that the introduction of Irish cattle should be denounced in a Parliamentary Act (Chas. II., 1668) as a "*nuisance*," and inhibited as such—"a nuisance" that one part of an empire should by its bounteous fertility be enabled to supply the others with a more plentiful supply of food! Yet such was the conclusion to which, by assuming false data, public opinion, the Legislature, and the statesmen of the day had logically arrived.

It was in vain that the illustrious Ormonde, whose admirable sense and patriotic feeling seemed to have carried him beyond the "ignorant present" of his own times, in the debate upon this Bill, among other things, pointed out that "the present trade between England and Ireland was extremely to the advantage of the former kingdom, which received provisions or rude materials in return for every species of manufacture; that if the cattle of Ireland were prohibited, the inhabitants of that island had no other commodity by which they could pay England for their importations, and must have recourse to other nations for a supply; that the industrious inhabitants of England, if deprived of Irish provisions, which made living cheap, would be obliged to augment the price of labour, and thereby render their manufactures too dear to be exported to foreign markets; that by cutting off almost entirely the trade between the kingdoms, all the natural bonds of union were dissolved, and nothing remained to keep the Irish in their duty but force and violence, and that by reducing that kingdom to extreme poverty, it would be even rendered incapable of maintaining that military power by which, during its well-grounded discontents, it must necessarily be retained in subjection."*

The king, says Hume, was convinced of the justness of these reasons, but the Commons were resolute in their purpose. In other words, the

* See Hume's History of England, chap. lxiv..

plain good sense of Ormonde, who had in a few simple sentences concentrated at once the now established fundamental principle of all sound commercial policy, and the true means of effecting a union between England and Ireland to the evident advantage of both, was unavailing against the public opinion of the day, based upon theories which were, no doubt, then considered more scientific and refined, and sharpened by the unfounded jealousy which arose from a belief in them. It seems, indeed, to the student of "The Wealth of Nations," difficult to believe that a principle so obviously false, as that the general prosperity of a kingdom could by possibility be furthered by the suppression or discouragement of a part of its own productive power, could ever have prevailed in any country. But the declaration that the production of cheap cattle was a "nuisance" involves an absurdity no less striking. The delusion, nevertheless, long subsisted, if, indeed, it can be said to be yet totally dispelled.

At the very time at which the remarks of the Duke of Ormonde above cited were made, a cotemporary statesman, who enjoyed a reputation very much superior to that of Ormonde as regarded skill in negotiation, learning, and literary capacity —Sir William Temple—makes, in an otherwise excellent tract upon Irish commerce, and one in which he appears throughout to be animated with the most friendly feelings towards Ireland, the following strange exception in *favour* of the very measure which Ormonde had ineffectually opposed :—

" In this survey one thing must be taken notice of as peculiar to this country, (Ireland), which is, that, as in the nature of its government, so, in the very improvement of its trade and riches, it ought to be considered not only in its own proper interest, but likewise in its relation to England, *to which it is subordinate,* and upon whose weal, in the main, that of this kingdom (*i.e.* Ireland) depends ; and, therefore, a *regard must be had of those points wherein the trade of Ireland comes to interfere with any main branches of the trade of England; in which cases the encouragement of such trade ought to be either declined or moderated, and so give way to the interest of trade in England, upon the health and vigour whereof the strength, riches, and glory of his Majesty's Crown seem chiefly to depend.*" *

This notion, nevertheless, continued to furnish the guiding maxim of the commercial policy of England as regarded Ireland, till a very late period. The doctrine which declared that the importation of Irish cattle was a nuisance soon afterwards declared Irish wool contraband. Then, as a last resort, the Irish betook themselves to manufacturing the raw wool ; but this was immediately

---

* Essay on the Advancement of Trade in Ireland, 1673.— *Temple's Works,* vol. iii.

suppressed, and Irish commerce, already crippled, was at last totally destroyed. The spirit which animated, or rather supported, the Irish through so many adversities was completely broken, and the restrictions under which their trade was laid were so insurmountable, that no attempt was made to resuscitate it. Trade with the Colonies was also debarred, it having been enacted by the Navigation Laws that Ireland was not to export or import any goods to or from the Colonies, except through England. Thus every avenue was effectually closed against Ireland, by measures which aimed exclusively at protecting the commercial prosperity of Great Britain.

It was not until the year 1780 that this commercial penal code began to be relaxed. Then, by the bold exertion of national spirit, roused and led on by the eloquence of Grattan, of Flood, and of Curran, great concessions were obtained. A subserviency to the selfish commercial system of England, however, still distinguished the Irish Parliament.* But more liberal views were beginning to prevail, and the Union in 1800, although excepting for a time certain important articles, nominally gave to Ireland a free trade. In the year 1806, another step was made, and free trade in corn with England was established (46 Geo. III., cap. 97), and at last, in the year 1826, all cross

* See "Newenham's Statistical and Historical Inquiry into the population of Ireland."

channel duties were abolished* and the commercial union of the countries was effected.

Without, therefore, ignoring the influence of the earlier events of Irish history upon its present condition, the year 1826 may be considered as an epoch from which a more detailed examination of the various measures, political, commercial, and economical, which were adopted by the Imperial Government towards Ireland, become more interesting, as being the consequences of an important principle, namely, the complete union of the component parts of the two kingdoms, which may be said to have been then for the first time practically acknowledged.

* Coals excepted. The tax on coal was not abolished until 1832, by the 2 William IV., cap. 21.

CHAPTER II.

Ireland in 1825.

Before proceeding to give an account of the measures adopted by the Imperial Government, it is necessary to describe the state of the country at the time of the recognition of this principle of the unity of the two kingdoms.

The condition of the population of Ireland in and about the year 1825 was far from being prosperous. Among the many causes which have been suggested as explanations of this, there appear to us to be two which are more particularly worthy of consideration, and which are intimately connected one with the other—the *first* is the minute division of the land held by the peasantry, and the *second* is the peculiar nature of the crop which formed the principal means of their subsistence, viz., the potato.

Turning our attention then first to the land, we

find that about this time it was owned by a comparatively small number of persons, and that while the properties were large, the holdings or farms were small.

A great sub-division of it had by degrees come about. This was partly owing to an hereditary tendency, for there had long existed in Ireland the custom of dividing the paternal property among all the members of a family, the natural result of which, as Mr. Blackburn expressed it, had been that " the sub-division of land and the multiplication of the species had gone on *pari passu.*" *

But the practice had also been encouraged by other circumstances. In the year 1793, an Act had been passed extending to every person possessed of a forty shilling freehold the right of voting for members of Parliament.

The creation of Parliamentary interest thus became an object, at first confined to the highest, but quickly extending itself to other classes. Landlords, considering that every freehold they created added so much to their personal and political interest in the country, often, on the expiration of a lease, cut up their farms into several smaller holdings, for the purpose of multiplying voters, and encouraged their leaseholders to divide their land for the same purpose.

---

* See evidence given before the Committee of the House of Commons to inquire into the state of Ireland, 1824-25.

Even political adventurers, to possess themselves of Parliamentary influence, purchased or leased large tracts of uncultivated land, and let it out in small lots to tenants, who reclaimed it and became freeholders. The farmer also, for the sake of creating voters, divided his land among his children, each of whom at the first opportunity again sub-divided his holding. Thus the continual sub-division of property was made subservient to political passion, and a continually increasing impetus was given to the process.

The manner in which this sub-division had been brought about was not the least of its evils, namely, the practice of sub-letting, to which for many years there had been great inducements.

It had been the practice of most landlords, and particularly of those who did not reside in the country, to grant leases for long terms and for large portions of their properties, to some individual on whom they relied for the payment of their rents, endeavouring thus to secure to themselves the advantages, whilst freeing themselves from the responsibilities attaching to the ownership of land; and as the difficulty of managing landed properties and of collecting rents had always been great, in consequence of the country continuing from various causes to be disturbed, there was naturally a strong inducement for landed proprietors to follow this course. The population, too, had rapidly increased, while the repression of the manufacturing interest had directed the whole physical energy of the nation to the cultivation of land, the minute division of which, excluding the possibility of a labouring class, rendered the possession of a portion of the soil, the only means by which subsistence was to be obtained.

Through the great demand thus arising the rate of rents rose, and a margin was left between the original rent of a farm and the price which it would fetch in the market.

The great war with France and free trade in corn with England rendered the prices of agricultural produce unnaturally high. Persons accordingly holding land under long leases, which they had obtained when rents were low, were now able to re-let it at high rents, and thus, without any labour or productive exertion whatever, to realize a profit. Those, again, who thus rented the land, as soon as they found they could make a profit by re-letting it, immediately did so, and in this way it passed through several hands, creating a class of intermediate proprietors known by the name of middlemen.

During the long war this practice of sub-letting grew so common, that land was let and re-let five, six, or even eight times, placing over a farm six or eight intermediate proprietors, and leaving to the actual cultivator little or nothing more than would barely support existence.

All these circumstances, therefore—hereditary usage, political interest, and sub-letting—combined to bring about that minute sub-division, which in some parts of the country appears to have reached to such a degree, that those who had the best opportunities of judging, agreed that it was materially impossible for the holdings to be further divided.*

Irrespective of sub-letting, there was another system very generally in use, but more particularly in Munster, namely, the holding a farm "in common," or in joint-tenancy. According to this practice, it was held by several different families, who were conjointly responsible for the rent. This combined in a strange manner the evils of minutely divided property with those of communism, and imposed a positive check upon industry, for the industrious occupier was often compelled to fulfil the engagements of the idle or unthrifty, who either neglected or were unable to contribute anything to the common stock.†

---

* Comns. Ctee. on Ireland, 1824-25.

† "The peculiar system adopted in most parts of Ireland in sub-dividing land, added much to the evils necessarily accompanying the existence of holdings so minute as those which the practice of sub-division had created. Instead of each sub-tenant, or assignee, of a portion of a farm receiving his holding in one compact lot, he obtained part of each particular quality of land, so that his tenement consisted of a number of scattered patches, each too small to be separately fenced, and exposed to

So long as the war lasted, and prices of land and food were high, things went smoothly enough. As the population increased, the increasing prices obtainable for what they produced, to some extent satisfied their wants, and the country was comparatively prosperous.

"Those," says Archbishop Doyle, adverting to this period, in one of his well-known letters, signed J. K. L., "who dwelt in caverns and the caves of the earth came forth, many of them from their lurking places, and raised huts which were at least visible. They procured clothing, and appeared abroad to swell the congregations, from which they were often absent through necessity. Chapels were also erected; and tracts of land, which before looked like a desert, put on the appearance of an inhabited country." (Letter 5.)

The basis of this prosperity was temporary and unreal; but its want of foundation was not noticed, until Napoleon was overthrown, and

the constant depredations of his neighbours' cattle, thus affording a fruitful source of quarrels, and utterly preventing the possibility of the introduction of any improved system of husbandry." (Digest of Evidence given before the Land Occupation Commisioners, 1845.)

This was called holding "*in rundale.*" In the evidence given before the Commissioners there is an account of a man in the County Donegal, (a tailor by trade,) who held his farm in *forty-two* different places, and at last gave it up in despair, declaring that it would take a very keen man to find it. There is an instance also of one field of half an acre of oats being held by twenty-two different persons.

peace declared, when a sudden and great fall in the prices of agricultural produce took place. The occupiers of land became no longer able to pay the rents at which they had taken it; the true state of affairs forced itself on public attention, and the misery and nakedness of the land became visible. For a time middlemen exacted the full rents from their tenants, but the depreciation of agricultural produce continuing, the immediate occupiers found it impossible to meet such demands, and as a natural result many of the middlemen, having little other property than that derived from the tenantry, became unable to make good the engagements they had entered into with the landlords, and were obliged to part with their interest in the land they had sub-let.*

Many thus became utterly ruined, all impoverished, and the country covered with a people who had grown up under circumstances totally different from those in which they now found themselves —the high prices which had rendered them comparatively prosperous had passed away, but they

* There was not much necessity for a reduction of the rents of land let before the year 1792, but the rents of land leased after that time had to be, and were reduced. Yet even then the rents exacted were frequently above what the produce would authorize; they had not, in fact, been lowered in a proportion adequate to the general depression; the demand for land being so great, and the competition for it so keen, that high rates were still obtainable.

themselves had not passed away; an impetus had been given to the population which did not cease when the war ceased, and the land was crowded to such a degree, as in many places to reach the limit of what it would support.

As this became more and more apparent, the idea gradually gained ground with the landowners that they had been acting on erroneous principles. Feeling already some of the evils of an over-abundant population, they foresaw the greater evils that must necessarily ensue in the event of its further increase, and a general impression was produced in the minds of all persons, that unless some change were made, a mass of pauperism would be accumulated, which the entire produce of the land could not feed.

But the evil effects of sub-division and sub-letting were not confined to bringing about an increase of population. The modes of agriculture consequent upon such small holdings deteriorated, production diminished, and the way was paved for that misery with which the next quarter of a century was fraught, culminating in the famine of 1846, and that visitation, attributable, no doubt, in great measure to natural causes beyond the control of human policy, became to Ireland a disaster of incalculable magnitude, falling, as it did, on a country which, by a long course of mismanagement, had been deprived of all those internal resources by which nations more fortunately situated have been enabled to pass through and survive such ordeals.

As leases which had been made some twenty or thirty years previously began to fall in, landlords found on their farms, in some instances, ten times the number of persons that had been there when the leases were made. Moreover, those to whom the land had in the first instance been let were men of substance; the tenants now found upon it were the very reverse, in fact, in the majority of instances, they were persons who had sunk to the lowest degree of indigence.

Sub-division had so evidently led to such great evils, that it was hoped that the opposite course, *consolidation*, would prove the appropriate remedy.

By the consolidation of farms, and the ejectment of the excess of tenantry, scope, it was expected, would be given for a better system of agriculture, leading to a greater certainty in the yield of the potato crop, an improvement in the quality of the soil, and the quantity of its produce. Solvent and respectable tenants, it was thought, would replace paupers, and a race of yeomanry, hitherto totally deficient, would be created.

The commencement of this great experiment, therefore, was made shortly after the conclusion of the war with France; and the account of its progress takes a prominent position in the social history of Ireland from that time down to the present. Upon it hinge, as it were, all the changes which have taken place in the state of the country—changes which, combined, may be said to amount to a social revolution.

The impediments in the way of carrying it out were at first almost insuperable. Independent of the resistance of the people, the state of the law afforded little assistance—great difficulty existing in getting an effective clause put into leases forbidding sub-letting, the Courts of Justice deciding generally against the validity of such clauses. In fact, it was nearly impossible, under the directions of the judges and the verdicts of juries, to obtain any forfeiture or penalty for sub-letting. But by degrees the wisdom of consolidation became generally recognized, and several Acts of Parliament were passed in the ten years after the peace, giving to the landlords increased facilities for ejecting the superabundant tenantry.

Different circumstances, too, were beginning to have some influence on the larger and wealthier proprietors. The people had by degrees attained a knowledge of the weight and the political influence the freehold gave them; the profit derived by the freeholder from his lease had become so insignificant that he despised the threats of his landlord, and voted against him, and landlords thus became aroused to the danger in which the 40s. freeholder placed them in elections, and an additional stimulus was thus given to consolidation.

When landlords saw, too, that both rent and property were likely to be swallowed up by an ever-increasing pauper population, they were determined, if they possibly could, to avert such a disastrous result. Hitherto they had lacked the inclination to prevent sub-letting, but they now found that they lacked the power—the system of granting long leases having placed the property out of their control—the continual sub-letting of it having removed the actual occupier far from their influence. This defect, as far as the future was concerned, was, however, remedied in the year 1826, by an Act of Parliament, known as the Sub-letting Act, which afforded facilities for carrying into effect the new course of action that had been determined on, and the principal clauses and effects of which we will discuss hereafter.

In the year 1825 many landlords were already trying to get rid of the middlemen, whom they found to be most pernicious to their interests, as well as to those of their tenantry. The system out of which they had arisen was obviously disadvantageous both to the proprietor and the cultivator, being one under which the former received the lowest, and the latter paid the highest rate of rent. It moreover made it utterly impossible for the landlord to take any steps for improving his property or the condition of his tenantry. It is true, that there was little accumulation of capital among Irish land-owners; but even those who had any were naturally unwilling to employ it in a manner which would have simply led to a demand by the middleman for a higher rent on account of the increased value of the holding, and thus while the middleman profited, the unfortunate tenant would remain as badly off as before, and the landlord receive no return for his outlay.

At this time, the value of land in Ireland was regulated by the quantity and degree of competition for it, and not upon a calculation of its probable produce, which in other countries would have been considered the true criterion of its value. The great demand consequently made those who had it to let masters of the situation, and in many parts of the country it was let "by cant"—*i.e.*, to the highest bidder. The middleman, by this means, obtained the promise of a high rent, and having done so, practised a most severe and arbitrary mode of exacting the payment of it.

Nor could he be expected to be influenced by any other consideration than that of extracting the largest possible amount of rent, regardless altogether of its proportion to the produce, for he well knew that he had only a temporary interest, and one liable to the changes of the times.

With little character and less interest, he exercised more authority and demanded more submission from his tenants than the real landlords. His characteristics have been described as " servility to his superiors, and tyranny towards his inferiors."*

The tenants holding land from him had no security, and derived little or no profit from their possession. They paid more than the average rate of rent; they gave labour under the average rate of labour, and they racked the land to exhaustion, either in the expectation of getting it cheaper when their term expired, or in the probability of being ejected from it, and getting the most out of it before they went.

The practices of middlemen are most admirably described in the following extract from "Castle Rackrent," which, though a work of fiction, presents a more faithful delineation of Irish customs and Irish life than is elsewhere to be found:—

"Rents must be paid up to the day and afore; no allowance for improving tenants; no consideration for those who had built on their farms. No sooner was a lease out, but the land was advertised to the highest bidder; all the old tenants turned out. All was now set at the highest penny to a parcel of poor wretches who meant to run away, and did so after taking two crops out of the ground. For let alone making English tenants (*i.e.*, a tenant who pays his rent the day it is due) of them every soul, he was always driving and driving, (*i.e.*, for rent,) pounding and pounding,

---

* See Castle Rackrent, by Miss Edgeworth.

and canting and canting, and replevying and replevying."

The legal power of landlords over their tenantry was considerable, but they being generally absentees their authority was either delegated to agents, or was wielded by each intermediate proprietor.

The landlord had (and still has) the right of distress—a power which was extended by an Act passed in the year 1817, giving permission to distrain the growing crops of the tenant in default of receiving payment of rent, although that crop was the subsistence for the ensuing year for the family of the tenant.

Upon the least reverse of prices, or any other circumstance which might disable the actual occupier from paying the full amount of the rent of his holding, the landlord (in which term is included each intermediate proprietor) was empowered by law to seize and sell to the highest bidder the cow, the bed, the potatoes in the ground, or any other property whatever in the possession of his tenant, without previous reference to any tribunal.

But the most effectual means by which he maintained his power over his tenants was by allowing them to fall into arrears of rent.

"Six months' credit," says Wakefield, in his Account of Ireland, " is generally given on the rents, which is called the ' hanging gale.'

" This is one of the greatest levers of oppression

by which the lower classes are kept in a kind of perpetual bondage ; for as every family almost holds some portion of land, and owes half a year's rent, which a landlord can exact in a moment, the debt hangs over their head like a load, and keeps them in a continual state of anxiety and terror. If the rent is not paid, the cattle are driven to the pound, and if suffered to remain there a certain number of days, they are sold."

Much of the neglected state of the peasantry must, no doubt, be attributed to absenteeism—a custom at every time prevalent amongst Irish land-owners.

The number of proprietors of land in Ireland has always been small as compared with the extent of the country, and the amount of the agricultural population, and of this number but a few have ever been constant residents on their own estates. Hence that want of personal attention to the condition of the tenantry, and the absence of that attachment and good-will which is so essential to the mutual interests of persons in the relation of tenant and landlord. The great proprietors of estates in England, who also possessed land in Ireland, naturally resided in the former country. Others who held estates in Ireland only, preferred the superior civilization, security, and luxury of England, and spent there the revenues they derived from their Irish property, indifferent to its management so long as they obtained its income.

Setting aside the question of absenteeism in its economic point of view, in its social view it is undoubtedly a great evil. There is the loss of the influence, and authority, and control which belong to education, rank, and property. By residing at home, landlords would have diffused a taste for improved methods of living, would have introduced better manners, would have set an example to their tenants and the lower classes, and would have taken care of their mutual interests. The absence of the proprietor of an estate might have been to some extent compensated for, had there been a resident agent; but even this was not common. There was no person, therefore, to give that superintendence which is essential on every landed property, to see that houses were not built unnecessarily, that improvement was going on, and to give encouragement where it was due. In the South of Ireland the principal part of the gentry had deserted their properties. The clergy of the Established Church even, were to some extent absentees, owing to their holding pluralities of livings, to a want of glebe-houses or other accommodation, and in some instances to a want of inclination to reside in their parishes; and the non-residence of a well-educated gentleman—of one able to do much good—was of great disservice to the country.

Left, to a great extent, to follow their own ideas, without guidance or without example, the people suffered accordingly. Distress was increased, owing to the want of employment, consequent on absenteeism; the tenantry of absentees were always in a worse condition than those of resident landlords, although it is true that many of the latter were embarrassed in their circumstances. Those, therefore, with whom the people came into immediate contact as regards dealings in land were generally middlemen—men of a class far below those who would afford a good example to the people—sometimes only appearing among them to collect the rents, and collecting them with great rigour and severity.

All blame must not, however, in this case be laid upon the one side. The conduct of the peasantry, and the state of affairs resulting therefrom, were not such as to induce landlords to become resident. Constant disturbances, varying only in degree, long existing animosities waiting only a favourable opportunity to be gratified, threatening letters, attempted or successful murders, were the ordinary phases of Irish country life, and aided materially in making landed proprietors shun this part of the kingdom for some other place where at least security was attainable.

From this description of the landed proprietors we must proceed to that of the lower orders of the people, for, at that time, Ireland possessed no middle class. Trade had been so long repressed that such a class did not exist in the towns, and the minute division of the land had prevented its growth in the country, the few who had prospered by trade during the war, had either raised themselves to higher positions, or, as more generally happened, had relapsed into their original state of depression.

CHAPTER III.

Condition of the Lower Classes in 1825.

The condition of the Irish peasantry in 1825 has been stated by eye-witnesses without number, to have been worse than that of any other in Europe.

One cause of this we have considered; and we shall now advert to what seems to us to have been the second cause, namely—the peculiar nature of the crop which formed the great means of their subsistence—the potato.

This is a crop which, upon the same space of ground, produces food for three times the number of people that wheat, rice, or any other description of grain could support. It is eminently wholesome and nutritious; and populations which may challenge a comparison with any other for stature, strength, and activity, are maintained in vigour by it alone, so long as the supply is plentiful. Its peculiar nature, moreover, enables it to be raised on soils so indifferent in quality, as to render any other crop upon such land impossible.*

What, then, at first sight appears more admirably adapted for the production and maintenance of a numerous, hardy, and contented people?

Yet, strange to say, these advantages are more than counterbalanced by circumstances which render a potato crop the most perilous of all supports, and which cause even its at times almost unbounded exuberance to be a danger instead of a blessing.

In the first place, it is eminently uncertain—a series of plentiful yields being often followed by scanty crops, or by partial or even total failure.

In the second place, the ill effects of this uncertainty are enhanced by the impossibility of storing it, for more than a very limited period. The potato can barely be preserved for a single year; thus the whole crop is consumed within that period, and the surplus of one year cannot make up for the deficiency of another. Accordingly, when there is the slightest failure, the price of this essential article of existence rises at once from one which allowed the population to revel in plenty of their favourite food, to one which almost denies them its use, or reduces them to starvation.

* The ridge or lazy bed universally adopted in its culture applied a system of drainage sufficient for one crop, without permanently draining the land, or extending any substantial benefit in that respect to the following crop.

And in like manner, as the deficiency of one year cannot be supplied by the plenty of another, so, before the present facilities of transport existed, the deficiencies of one place could not be supplied with the surplus of another, the great bulk and weight of this produce and the expense, often indeed almost the impossibility, of conveyance, being so great as to preclude the relief of a scarcity by importation from abroad, or even from neighbouring counties.

But the greatest disadvantage arising from an exclusive dependence on the potato, is that, being the cheapest description of food, the people are unable to purchase what is dearer when a failure occurs; there is no humbler fare to be fallen back upon, even for a time; the potato or famine is the alternative: so that a population, placing their entire reliance on this crop, are placed upon "the extreme verge of human subsistence," and the slightest deficiency causes a dearth.

The unprosperous condition of the Irish people arose, then, we believe, from two causes—(1) the sub-division of land; (2) the nature of the food of the peasantry; and they combined, brought about the great population which covered Ireland, and with that population a train of attendant evils.

The ease with which the miserable cabins and simple food were obtained, by removing all difficulties in obtaining sufficient support for a family, induced early marriages,* men frequently marrying at the age of sixteen, and girls even so young as that of fourteen.

The extreme poverty of the people prevented their taking such an interest in creating a respectable provision for themselves in life, as men possessed of any property always feel. Their state, they said, could not be more wretched when married than before ; and, moreover, they had, in marrying early, the special object of having children to support them in their old age. Where the head of a family was extremely poor, living in a wretched cabin, and having only one apartment where he and his children dwelt, and when his neighbour was similarly circumstanced, a constant intercourse was kept up in these small dwellings, so that the different sexes were thrown much together, and that respectful distance observed in families enjoying anything of comfort or position, was entirely lost amongst them.

The number of inhabitants of a country is everywhere affected by the facility or difficulty of

* It has been said, and tried to be proved by statistics, that early marriages tend less to increase population than marriages at a more advanced period of life, owing to the large number of children that die. As regards Ireland, however, this was not the case, for the people married early, and the marriages are more prolific there than in any other country, and it is a very common circumstance to see families of nine or ten children.

obtaining the means of subsistence,* and in Ireland, where great facilities existed for obtaining food, the population rapidly increased. Soon it had almost passed the supply; and to meet the demand, more and more land was put under potatoes until, ultimately, the whole of the lower orders subsisted entirely on that article of food.

All these circumstances, therefore, led in Ireland to the " boundless multiplication of human beings satisfied with the lowest condition of existence ;" and the rapidity with which this increase was effected, may be understood from the fact, that the population of the country doubled within thirty-three years.† It was, in fact, only limited by the difficulty of procuring food.

In many parts of the country, it appears that it would have been impossible for human beings to exist in a greater state of misery.

" In a parish with which I am connected," writes Archbishop Doyle, in one of his letters, to which we have already adverted, " consisting of about 8,000 souls, not less than 337 families were relieved as public paupers during the last year ; and probably one-half as many more, who would prefer death to the public exposure of their distress, suffered for nearly two months all the horrors of extreme want.

---

* See Malthus—" Essay on Population."
† By the year 1825, the population was more than 7,000,000.

" In another parish, six-sevenths of the population subsisted for months of the last year either on alms, or on one scanty meal of the most wretched food; and nearly all the moveables they possessed were sold or pledged, to provide them with this pittance."*

These are but illustrations of the extent and nature of the distress which pervaded the country.

To obtain a more vivid picture, however, of the condition of the people, we must follow them to their homes.

These were of the most miserable description. Houses they were not, but cabins, built of stones and mud, or mud alone; the roof made of a few beams of timber, and covered with straw or with a surface called scraws, often not even sufficient to prevent the rain from coming through; the floor consisting of the ground on which the cabin was built; generally speaking, no windows or chimneys, and but one small door; dens rather than cabins—dens of filth, disease, and misery.† In

---

* Letter XI.

† " I was remarkably struck," says a witness before the Committee of the House of Lords on Colonization, in 1847, " in passing through Roscommon, with very long ranges of buildings, and seeing the country in a very miserable condition. On making inquiry, I ascertained that each long pile of building had originally commenced with one house, or what is called a 'bay'— that is, as much as a plank would stretch across, covered over

these abodes, there was nothing that could be called furniture. It was a luxury to have a box to put anything into; it was a luxury to have what they called a dresser for laying a plate upon, or anything of that kind they might possess. Generally there was little beyond an iron cast metal pot and a milk tub. The entire family slept in the same apartment. They had seldom any bedsteads, and as to covering, they had generally nothing but straw, whilst some few possessed blankets. Their diet was equally wretched. Except on the sea coast, where fish was sometimes obtainable, it consisted of potatoes and water during the greater part of the year, and of potatoes and sour milk during the remainder.

The prevalence of fever and other epidemic diseases were the natural results of such circumstances.*

with some brambles and some rushes, occasionally with a thatch of straw. The son of the first inhabitant desired to marry, and he had another piece added to the tenement equal to his father's, and became a resident there. Another son or daughter married, and then another portion was added; then came grandchildren, and they made additions; then when the old man died, there was still some one to occupy his house, and those buildings went on increasing."

* The prevalence of contagious fever in Ireland, it may be observed, was a calamitous indication of the general distress of the peasantry, and the increase or decrease of fever, as ascertained by the admissions into the fever hospitals, was a criterion of the amount of distress the peasantry were undergoing.

The next above these cottier-tenants were the small farmers, holding from ten to thirty acres; but they were too poor to constitute a middle class, and had hitherto made common cause with those below them.

Their farming was of the most slovenly description, and the food for themselves and their dependents was still the potato. They built their own habitations, and repaired them at their own cost. Their selling produce, after paying the rent, afforded a little better clothing and a few more comforts than enjoyed by the cottier-tenants. Otherwise, there was no distinction between these classes. Nor was the system of agriculture which they pursued more conducive to the welfare of the country than that pursued by the cottiers. The latter brought nothing to the land but their own labour, and got nothing out of it but their own bare subsistence, whilst the former did but little more, investing in agriculture no capital, but conducting the husbandry by means of persons who drew the profits of their labour from the land immediately at their own risk and charge.

These two classes formed the peasantry of the country.

Much, doubtless, of the poverty which prevailed was to be attributed more immediately to the want of employment, which arose from the redundancy of labour. This is the natural consequence of a population larger than what is demanded by the capital or wealth of a country. By the creation of an enormous competition for labour its price is reduced, and the result is incomplete subsistence to those who can find employment—complete indigence for those who cannot.

The population was, in fact, so much beyond the demand for employment, that in some parts of the country one-half was stated to be without any. In Munster there was about 2,000,000 inhabitants, and employment for 1,000,000.* In other parts the disproportion was said to be still greater.

In the North of Ireland the linen manufacture employed a large number of persons, but in other parts of the country the cultivation of land was the only employment, and this could only be obtained from the larger farmers, and for a comparatively short season of the year. For seven out of the twelve months there was, perhaps, nothing to be done. Nor had the peasantry who produced their own crop much occupation, the potato cultivation requiring but little trouble, and affording only about six weeks' labour in the spring, and four in the autumn. In April generally the whole of the seed was put into the ground. For six or eight weeks afterwards nothing could be done; under proper management, the crop ought then to have been weeded and moulded, but the people seldom took this trouble. They sowed and they reaped, or

* See evidence given before the Select Committee of the House of Commons—1823—Poor in Ireland.

rather, they planted and they dug; and from the time in the autumn, when the crop was taken from the ground, until the following spring, when preparations had to be made for the new crop, the potato culture afforded no employment whatever. There existed, nevertheless, in the minds of the people a great anxiety for work. The peasantry of the South and West quitted their homes at particular times of the year in search of it, migrating even in large numbers to England at the harvest time, and returning to their homes to secure their own potato crops.

The great and rapid increase of population had not been accompanied by a corresponding increase of capital, which not only was insufficient to develop the resources of the country, but was not even enough for the requirements of daily life. Money was an article of which the Irish peasant knew but little. Scarcely any independent labourers received their wages in it, and the potato was not only the food of the labourer, but also constituted to a very great extent the agricultural currency of the country. The farmers were in the habit of paying wages by the well-known con-acre system, which, though it exercised a direct tendency to encourage early marriages, by procuring the labourer a supply of food, yet has been instrumental in bringing about the great and desirable transition from pauper cottier-tenants to independent labourers.

According to it, the farmer let a small portion of land, generally under an acre, for one season only, for the sole purpose of growing potatoes. He manured the ground, and prepared it to receive the seed, and then handed it over to the labourer. On this piece the latter grew the potato which was to be his supply of food for the next year, and for it he was nominally to pay so many pounds an acre, the rent generally given was from £8 to £10, sometimes as low as £5 per acre; but instead of paying this sum, he worked for a certain number of days for the farmer from whom he took the land, and thus did away with the necessity of the employment of money in the transaction. In consequence of the low rate of wages, the whole time of the labourer only just sufficed to make up the rent.

Then with the refuse of their miserable diet they contrived to feed a pig, which they sold for from 30s. to 60s., and so succeeded in obtaining some clothing. But this mode of life was precarious in the extreme, and it was upon people so situated that the slightest deficiency in the potato crop told with deadly effect.

The con-acre system of paying wages was, however, in many respects disadvantageous. To the peasantry it was always unsatisfactory, giving them a less immediate reward for their industry, and a less clear and intelligible mode of ascertaining that they were dealt with fairly; but as it resulted from their poverty, a change could not suddenly be made; and it was only as the transition of the peasantry from pauper cultivators to independent labourers was gradually effected, that this truck system was abandoned for the payment of money wages.

The want of capital in Ireland was attributable to many causes.

"Capital," say the Committee of 1823, in their Second Report on the state of the poor, "can only accumulate out of the savings of individuals. In Ireland there are few persons, who either in manufactures or agriculture, conduct their operations on such a scale as to admit of much surplus for accumulation. The only manufacture which flourishes, namely, the linen, is spread abroad amongst a population which, at the same time, cultivate the soil for their sustenance, and though such a system of manufacture may be more conducive to health and morals in the manufacturer, it is incompatible with large savings. In like manner, in agriculture, the tendency to subdivision of farms and the general practice of throwing the expense of buildings and repairs on the tenant, countervail the accumulation of profit in the hands of the farmer, and the application thereof to beneficial enterprise in agriculture."

This want was shown by the wretched description of implements used both in domestic manufactures and in agriculture, as well as by their general deficiency. The ploughs, carts, harrows, were of the rudest description, and the farmers had no accommodation either for themselves or to enable them to preserve and bring the produce of their farms to market in a proper state. It was shown, too, in the system of agriculture, which was very defective. There was no regular, or at least no beneficial, rotation of crops adopted; drainage was entirely neglected. "They have no capital," says Archbishop Doyle, speaking of the small farmers and cottiers, "they cannot drain, nor fence, nor manure their fields; they cannot improve their seed; their cattle are not able to work; it is not in their power to employ or feed labourers; they have no winter crops; their fallows are not stirred or cleansed; the most simple or useful improvement in husbandry is not within their reach."*

Such, then, was the physical and social condition of the lower classes, nor could it fail to have its effects upon their character and disposition. By the wretchedness they suffered, their minds were enervated, their energies paralyzed, and they were left incapable of useful exertion. They had no means of acquiring anything but a bare subsistence, and they looked no farther; they became cringing, servile, careless, and despondent. The want of regular work made them indolent. "I do not think," says a witness before the Committee

* Letter V. of J. K. L.

of 1830, "that these people could have become better, from the low degraded state of society in which they were; they never could have bettered themselves, as they had not a spirit of emulation."

Their intercourse with the outer world was restricted. Being the providers of their own wants, raising the food upon which they subsisted, trade and commerce could not arise, whilst the difficulties of communication with other countries, or even with the more enlightened parts of their own, prevented them participating in any progress which might have been made at this time. They were left accordingly in the most miserable state of ignorance and superstition—an ignorance not confined to the want of a knowledge of reading and writing, but extending itself to the commonest affairs of daily life.*

With all these failings, however, the Irish were not an immoral people, and in the lower classes many of those crimes, which are so conspicuous amongst the lower classes of other populations, are almost entirely unknown.

The whole country, however, was not in the deplorable condition above depicted; the state of the peasantry in parts of the North and of the East being superior both in houses, clothing, education, and general habits to those we have been describing.

* See evidence given before the Committees on Irish Poor in 1824-5 and 1830.

Never yet almost has a page been written on the subject of Ireland that allusion has not been made to her great natural resources. To the territory which she occupies the world can have access. " We look to her ports," says Archbishop Doyle, " they are safe and spacious ; to her rivers, they are deep and navigable ; to her position on the globe, and she seems to be intended as the emporium of wealth, as the mart of universal commerce."*

Abounding in all the riches which Nature can bestow, a temperate climate, a fertile soil, mineral wealth, and most valuable fisheries ; but abounding in vain. All these sources of employment which, had they been available, would have promoted both socially and morally the welfare of the people; all lying idle and unused. And why? Population had outrun capital.

Ireland had never been a wealthy country; and although at this time slowly and steadily progressing under greater freedom of commerce and increasing facilities of trade, yet the population had increased so rapidly, as not alone to neutralize the improvement, but to deluge the greater part of the country with poverty. And as each year went by, this evil was becoming greater—the struggle for existence was getting more fierce, the country more disturbed, life and property more

---

* Letter XI. of J. K. L.

insecure. Capitalists, who would have been unable to resist the temptation of quadrupling their wealth in the development of the resources of the country, now shunned the Irish shores, and carried to other, even to foreign lands, that which would have been the salvation of Ireland. Insecurity prevailed, and the venture was too great. And it was, indeed, too clearly evident, that until this order of things was reversed, Ireland could never raise herself into a prosperous country.

CHAPTER IV.

The Sub-Letting Act.

The great and apparently undue increase of the population, which had taken place in Ireland since the time of the French war, had, as we have seen, come to be looked upon, not unnaturally, as the principal source of the continued insecurity, poverty, and misery which afflicted the country. That it was the immediate cause of them, and that which forced itself upon the attention of every one, there can be no doubt; but it will be found upon closer examination, that its disastrous effect was principally owing to its combination with other causes, and to defects in the social organization, habits, and character of the people.

Among these, may be enumerated—a want of security for property and the fruits of industry, and its accumulations, consequent upon the political and religious dissensions to which we have already adverted, and to the almost entire want of *capital* for the employment of the labouring classes and the increase of the produce of the land, which was the natural result of that insecurity. To these, however true may be our love, or warm our admiration of the many high and brilliant gifts which adorn our countrymen, we cannot avoid adding certain traits of the national character, which are too strongly marked, and too general, notwithstanding numerous and honourable exceptions, not to be taken into account in any candid examination of its social condition. It is but too true, that the manners of the Irish gentry, and more especially that part of it immediately connected with the land, have been marked by reckless profusion and extravagance, by culpable carelessness of their own interests, and neglect of their tenants. So far were they, at the time we speak of, from being able to supply the want of capital to which we have adverted, that they were usually themselves deeply involved in pecuniary difficulties. Qualities, in themselves amiable, had with the Irish gentry become actually detrimental. Hospitality was pushed to riotous waste, and a love of sport to a neglect of every serious duty. Of absenteeism we have elsewhere spoken ; but of too many of the Irish absentees it may be observed, that not alone were they unable to supply that capital which was necessary, not merely for the increase, but for the preservation of their fortunes, but they were men usually living beyond their means, out of sight of the circumstances which were preparing their own ruin, and inflicting misery on their dependants.

Something of the same recklessness and improvidence has, it cannot be denied, ever pervaded the lower orders. Superior in intelligence to most populations, in the conduct of life they fall short of slower natures. A certain elasticity of animal spirits, which enables them to face misery gaily, and to bear it with patience and without despondency, is too predominant in their nature to be consistent with the foresight and plodding perseverance necessary for a permanent bettering of their condition. A power of averting their eyes from the dark side of things, is one which they, no doubt, possess in no common degree; nor is the philosophy a bad one if not used in excess; but in their situation it is lamentably opposed to improvement—above all, is but ill calculated to arrest that downward course to poverty, which it is so easy to pursue and so difficult to retrace. Drink was, and is, too often called upon to deaden the stings of misery for the moment, but only to sharpen them on the morrow. And this vice—marvellously checked for a time by the praiseworthy exertions of Father Mathew—was woven into the tissue of their other miseries, to the infinite aggravation of their deplorable effects.

The spectacle, however, which in consequence of the increased population forced itself on the attention of the Irish land-owner, was that of his estate incumbered by a too numerous pauper tenantry, insolvent as to his rents, and unable to produce from their small and ill-cultivated holdings even a bare subsistence of the lowest class of food for themselves and their ever-increasing families; while he, on the other hand, was without capital to employ the superabundant hands as labourers, and thus to provide that needful increase of food which the land, if better cultivated, might be expected to produce.

And what presented itself to him, and with truth, as the chief if not the only obstacle to this wished-for increase by more effectual cultivation? We have elsewhere referred to it: the minute sub-division of the land into separate holdings, occupied by paupers, without capital or efficient implements, cultivating (if it may so be called) the ground in small independent patches — a system of husbandry notoriously incapable of developing its fertility, or of producing a tithe of the crops that might be obtained under other management, which would enable it to maintain in comfort a population far greater than that which could then scarcely be said to exist upon its scanty produce.

The necessity of a change from the system of small holdings to that of larger farms, in order to develop agricultural produce, is not one peculiar to Ireland; for it has been felt in almost every country which has advanced to a certain degree of civilization, and in many instances was resorted to long before the population had increased to the degree to which it afterwards attained, and which, under proper management, the land was found capable of maintaining. In many parts of Germany this change had been going on; and a reference to the historians in the time of James I. and Elizabeth will show that in this respect the condition of the peasantry of England in the sixteenth century was very similar to that of Ireland at the time we now-speak of. Great poverty was felt, evidently from the insufficiency of the produce under the system of small, independent holdings at that time prevailing, to maintain the then existing population, which, it need scarcely be remarked, did not amount to a third part of that which the same land *now* supports in affluence. The same remedy—a severe one—which has of late times been applied in Ireland, was then found necessary in England. The same sufferings which accompanied the transition from the one to the other in Ireland in our day, were then felt in England, and let us hope that the same beneficial results will ultimately be attained.

A passage to be found in an account of England, by the most illustrious as well as the most benevolent of the statesmen of that day—Sir Thomas More, a trustworthy witness on such a subject—contains at once so graphic a picture of what then occurred in that country, and one which so strikingly resembles what has so often been seen in Ireland, that we cannot refrain from quoting it :—

" They must needs depart away, poor, wretched souls—men, women, husbands, wives, fatherless children, widows, woful mothers with their young babes, and the whole household, small in substance, much in number; away they trudge out of their known and accustomed houses, finding no place to rest in. All their household stuff, which is very little worth, though it might well abide the sale—yet, being suddenly thrust out, they be constrained to sell it for a thing of nought ; and when they have wandered about till that be spent, what can they do but steal, and then *pardi* be hanged, or else go about a-begging."

The remedy in England proved efficient, but it is evident that the sufferings entailed by its application were of a nature similar, if not equal in extent, to those experienced here.

The obvious, and indeed the only practicable course which could suggest itself under these circumstances to an Irish landlord, who wished to avert his own ruin, and to check the ever-growing misery of his tenantry, was to get rid of the redundant pauper occupiers of the small holdings, and to substitute persons able to cultivate to better purpose the land consolidated into larger farms. To this, accordingly, the landed proprietors had recourse—each for himself, endeavouring, by ejecting the small holders from their tenements, to relieve the estate from its pauper population. The obstacles which opposed themselves to the execution of this plan, and the misery which it entailed, may be conceived, but cannot easily be overrated.

It is obvious that, although the operation of reducing the pauper population by forcing them to go elsewhere, may have appeared to be successful on any particular estate, the sum of human misery in the country at large was not thereby diminished as to number, and was certainly in the first instance increased in intensity; the means, as we have said, being insufficient to employ any great number of the ejected cottiers as labourers on the lands they had held as tenants.

Emigration had not come, nor could it immediately come, to relieve the burthen; neither did a Poor Law at that time exist, even if such provision would have been adequate to meet the demands which would have been made upon it. Unoccupied or waste lands, upon which to form new settlements, there were, but the capital necessary to reclaim them was nowhere to be found.

Hordes of homeless wanderers were thrown loose upon the country, who, urged by the pangs of want to the crimes which want suggests, and at the same time burning with resentment under the sense of injury, too often wreaked a fearful revenge upon those whom they regarded as the authors of their woes, or on those whom they thought had profited by their wrongs. The landlord and the new tenants of the farms from which they had been ejected, were equally the objects of their hatred; and the terror felt by these latter of the wild justice by which they were liable to be overtaken, added another element of horror to the situation. The shadowy beings which the poet describes as ever watching by the infernal gate—

> "Metus et malesuada Fames et turpis Egestas
> Terribiles visu formæ! Letumque Labosque,"*

may be said to have stalked through the land in hideous reality at this period of its history.

A resolution to follow the plan of consolidation became at last so general as to have ripened into a policy, which in the year 1826 received the sanction of the Legislature, in the Act of Parliament called the Sub-Letting Act. (7 Geo. IV., cap. 28.)

This Act prohibited the sub-letting of property by a lessee, unless with the express consent of the proprietor—(a consent not likely to be obtained, except in very extraordinary cases)—and thus it was calculated to restrain the ever-multiplying minute division of land, which had been the ruin of the country, and to give land-owners the power

> *"Fear, crime-persuading Hunger, squalid Want,
> Forms terrible to view! with Death and Toil."

of gradually improving their properties and the condition of their tenantry.

The tendency to consolidation already existing previous to the passing of the Act, gave landlords an increased desire to avail themselves of the powers conferred by law, and thus brought it into practical use almost immediately.

When a farm fell out of lease, invariably in the miserable and wretched state before described, both as regarded the occupiers and the land, measures were taken for the removal of the pauperized tenants. They were served with notice to quit, and if they did not give up possession, steps were taken for their eviction under the new Civil Bill Ejectment Act. The land was then thrown into larger holdings, which were let to those who had at least some little capital, and who would be able to cultivate larger farms. With such it fared, indeed, in some respects better, but with those ejected, how sad was their lot!

The miserable beings dislodged from their abodes found themselves with but small resources and with no refuge. At first they generally made an attempt to establish themselves on the next estate, taking, when they could, fresh patches of mountain land, which they reclaimed, and upon which they built their cabin. If that expedient failed, they moved to a neighbouring town in search of employment, but as that, however, was seldom obtainable, they soon spent the trifling pecuniary means derived from the remission of their rents, and the sale of the stock which their landlords relinquished; and then existence was but barely supported by the assistance of charity.

But not alone were those that had been evicted rendered miserable. They carried with them and propagated that misery; for the suburbs of the towns became crowded with these poor creatures, who either swarmed into the houses already built, instances being known of from four to seven families living in one cabin with two rooms,* or built hovels alongside of the road, and became what were known as "squatters." In these places was beheld the "misery and suffering which no language can describe, and which it is necessary to witness in order fully to estimate."

"They increased the stock of labour, they rendered the habitations of those who received them more crowded, they gave occasion to the dissemination of disease, and they were obliged to resort to theft and all manner of vice and iniquity."†

In their abodes of wretchedness and filth, disease was produced by extreme want; it wasted the people, because they had no food or comforts to restore them, and it was no uncommon circumstance for them actually to die of hunger.

---

* Report of Committee on Poor in Ireland, 1832.
† Evidence of Dr. Doyle before ditto.

It must not be supposed, however, that all evictions were effected in the harsh manner in which it has been the habit to describe them. In many instances the landlords gave those whom they turned away the means of emigrating; and in later years some even sent out whole ships full of their former tenantry to America. In the majority of cases arrears of rent were remitted, heavy debts were forgiven, and the tenants were allowed to sell whatever little stock they possessed, so that they might have some means to begin life with again. It is, however, undeniable that the removal of the poor occupiers from their dwellings and the land which they had long held, was the cause of intense suffering, and there occurred doubtless many cases of great hardship, where persons were evicted in a manner wholly regardless of humanity and justice. One such case was sufficient to rouse the anger and stimulate the hatred of the people; and it was partly from the fear felt by the landlords that a too rapid series of evictions would lash the people into uncontrollable fury, and partly from motives of humanity, that the clearance of estates did not proceed quicker. There was nothing that the people would not forgive sooner than turning them from the place where their fathers and grandfathers had lived, from the cabin which they themselves had built, from the farm "round every sprig of which every string of their heart was twined."

By slow degrees some of the land was cleared, and the advantages of such a course became apparent. But, however desirous landlords might have been to accomplish these clearances rapidly, the occasions in which they could be effected arose only when the leases expired; and as much land had been leased by land-owners for a long term, it was evident that many years must elapse before the consolidation system could be carried into effect throughout the whole country.

The progress of the transition, too, was all the slower from the fact that there were two ways in which land became sub-divided—the first by sub-letting, the second by sub-dividing. The Sub-Letting Act affected only the former; to prevent the latter by enactment would have been scarcely possible. Indeed, there was no duty connected with the management of property more difficult to be performed than the prevention of sub-division. The feeling of the people was strongly opposed to such a restriction, and every sympathy enlisted against the landlords who endeavoured to enforce it.

And now, in criticizing this great measure, we must observe, that it should be judged not alone by the effects it produced, but by those evils which it unquestionably warded off. If, as is usually done by the Irish peasantry themselves, it is judged simply by the fearful amount of misery entailed in the removal of the poor from the land, the measure must be pronounced one of the most cruel acts of selfishness and tyranny ever adopted, and one which could not fail to excite in those who were the sufferers, feelings of hatred and animosity to the Government and to the higher orders. They were unable to understand how such a procedure could be for the general advantage of the country; they could not see why they should be made the victims, or why others should profit by their sufferings. Viewed in their light, it was but another act of rapacity on the part of the landlords—of tyranny on the part of the British Government.

But although the present evils it entailed were so great, the advantages resulting from the system, pursued under its sanction, were, on the other hand, very considerable and ever-increasing. Improvements of all kinds in agriculture, increase of produce, and consequent amelioration in the condition of the people—all, before long, developed themselves in those places where the new system was carried into effect. And these effects, as they became general, more than counterbalanced the misery which had at first followed, and which was unhappily the unavoidable result of this policy.

Most of all, however, we must bear in mind the indisputable fact that such a measure had become an imperative necessity if Ireland was not to be overwhelmed in ruin. All the most distinguished men of the day were agreed upon this.

" Had sub-division gone much further," said Dr. Doyle,* "the misery would have of necessity increased. It was, indeed, *essentially necessary* for the good of the country that the system should be corrected, and every wise man applauds those measures which were taken for the correction of it."—(Evidence before Select Committee on the State of the Poor in Ireland, 1830.)

And the Commissioners appointed to inquire into the state of the poor in Ireland in 1830, in their report say :—

" In making the change, in itself important and salutary, a fearful extent of suffering was produced, but *the change was unavoidable,* and could not have been delayed; a postponement could not have averted the evil day which would eventually have come, and been attended with pressure aggravated by reason of the postponement."

In the sight of the misery consequent on this measure, there was the one consolation, that the suffering then entailed was only a part of what must inevitably have taken place had a change in the system of managing land not been made. If sub-division had continued, the people would constantly have been increasing in numbers, and sinking in condition, until a famine, in comparison with which the famine of 1846 would have appeared small, must have occurred.

* Roman Catholic Bishop of Kildare and Leighlin.

At the period when the old system was superseded, it was producing vast suffering and misery, and by anticipating the inevitable effects of the habits of the people, it was thought that the suffering would be mitigated. The treatment was a rude one, and the suffering entailed made it seem doubly cruel from being authoritatively applied. For such a disorganized state of society, however, it was the only one that could be devised. It was the infliction on the country of an immediate and terrible evil, for the prevention of a still greater, irremediable evil, and for the securing of a future and permanent good—it was the purchase of the existence of a nation, by a sacrifice of part of its population.

The existence of a provision for the poor, or of any means except casual charity by which their sufferings could have been alleviated, would, it is thought, at this time have been very desirable. Indeed, the principle of giving aid from a public fund to a removed tenant was not only justifiable, but was also to a certain extent called for, by the fact of the Legislature having directly and indirectly interfered, and made no inconsiderable change in the condition of the poorest land-occupiers by the passing of several Acts of Parliament.*

But no such provision existed, not even any

---

* See Report of Committee on Poor in Ireland, 1832.

organized system for the collection and distribution of charitable funds, and the poor were left entirely to their own resources.

The following extract from the Report of the Railway Commissioners in 1838 treats of this part of the subject so ably, that we cannot refrain from quoting it :—

"The proprietors of estates," say they, "claim public support in their endeavours to bring the country to a sound and secure condition, by opposing and counteracting the further progress of so ruinous a system (sub-division), and if they would proceed in all cases with discretion, and a just consideration of those whose interests are as nearly concerned as their own, they are entitled to it. Of course, we do not palliate the injustice and the cruelty of turning families adrift, helpless and unprotected, upon the world. There is a compact, implied at least, between the landlord and the peasantry who have been brought up on his estate, by which the latter have as good a right to protection, as the lord of the soil has to make arbitrary dispositions for the future management of his property. Nor do we think that it makes much difference as to the force of this obligation, whether the injurious sub-division of lands was made by the direct sanction and for the immediate benefit of the tenant in fee, or by others to whom the power of a landlord over the property has been delegated by lease. It is not denied that

F

those sub-divisions were lawful at the time they were made. They were a part of the system then recognised, and in operation for the management of property; for their effects, therefore, upon the general welfare and security, the property itself is justly to be held accountable. Nor is this responsibility to be shuffled aside, or laid at the door of persons who, having ceased to possess an interest in the land, are no longer in a state to repair the error that has been committed; but the country will look to those who now hold the property, having received it charged with all its moral as well as its legal engagements. Still, however, as the land-holders or owners of estates are really unable to sustain the whole of this liability, and to proceed at the same time with that work of improvement which is so essential for the interest of all classes of the community, and eventually of none more than of the labouring poor, it is much to be desired, as an object of public importance, that means be taken speedily to distribute part of the burthen through other channels."—(Railway Commissioners' Second Report, 1838. By Drummond.)

It was with this view that different plans were suggested which, it was thought, would help to carry the country through the transition, but which, one after another, failed or were abandoned; and until the year 1840, when the Poor Law came into operation, no measure sufficiently general to have any effect was adopted, and the people were left to shift for themselves as best they could.

We have dwelt thus long upon this subject, for it is the turning point in the history of Ireland; and a clear comprehension of it is of the utmost importance to enable us to understand other social changes which have taken place, and which were but consequences of the policy here described.

CHAPTER V.

Administration of Justice.

It is a trite remark, but a true one, that there is no more unfailing criterion of the degree of happiness and civilisation of a country, than the justice of its laws, combined with the efficacy of their administration.

A poet has said with regard to Governments—

> " On forms of Government let fools contest ;
> Those best administered are still the best."—Pope.

And if there is any practical sagacity in the observation, as regards the conflicting opinions which have ever divided mankind upon the subject of political rule, it certainly may be applied with even still greater truth to what relates to criminal or civil jurisprudence. The strict *administration* of the laws is the condition without which the purpose or the wisdom of the legislator will be unavailing.

In no country has the "administration of justice" been more fitted to call forth such a reflection than in Ireland. In none does it present stranger anomalies, in few has it suffered from greater irregularities, and nowhere have greater difficulties been opposed to its effectual reformation.

It has been said, and it must be presumed not without truth, by a high legal authority, while in the exercise of the highest functions in the system upon which he comments:—

"There exist in this country (Ireland) two sorts of justice, the one for the rich, the other for the poor, both equally ill-administered."

Such is the deliberate opinion expressed by Lord Redesdale, when Lord Chancellor of Ireland. And if we place beside it that of an English Chancellor of no mean capacity (Lord Brougham)— "In England, justice is delayed, but, thank Heaven, it can never be sold; in Ireland, it is sold to the rich, refused to the poor, and delayed to all"—we need not recur to other authorities to determine what has been thought of the general character of the administration of justice in this country.

And yet, strange to say, the first observation which offers itself to an inquirer is, that the laws of Ireland are in themselves nearly identical with those of England—the methods of procedure by which they are carried into execution are the same, the constitution of the tribunals in the two countries in no way differs, and, moreover, the legal maxims and rules of practice acted upon traditionally in English courts of justice, are not less known or recognised in the courts of Ireland.

It need scarcely be added, that as a body of jurisprudence, reduced by immemorial usage to an assured system of practice, there does not exist a code of law more honest in its purposes, more efficient in its action, or more careful of individual rights and liberties, than that of England, *as there administered.* Such defects as may attach to it in common with all human institutions, are the object of careful correction whenever they become apparent; but they have seldom been such as to have interfered with a ready compliance with its decisions, or a firm reliance on its general purity and justice.

How, then, are we to account for the fact—but too notorious—that *this very* body of laws, as *administered in Ireland,* has been attended with opposite consequences?

Here, habitual veneration has been replaced by habitual disrespect; reliance, by incurable distrust; and cheerful submission too often by violent resistance. What is looked up to in England as a safeguard and protection against wrong, is in Ireland hated as an engine of oppression—by Englishmen to be under the law's rebuke is felt to be a disgrace, in Ireland it is in most cases regarded as an honour, or courted as a martyrdom.

The questions which present themselves, therefore, are—first, Why has this been so? and second, How can it be amended?

To these it is difficult to offer satisfactory replies. They, nevertheless, must ever call for anxious inquiry on the part of anyone who feels a real interest in the welfare of his country.

Laws unsuited to the moral condition of a people are proverbially of little use—

> " Quid leges sine moribus
> Vanae proficiunt "—

is a maxim which expresses one of the profoundest truths of political jurisprudence. Assigning to " mores" its most extended signification—as not only pointing to the morals, but the temper, habits of thought, traditional feelings, and prejudices of a people—the aphorism will apply to the case of Ireland, and furnish us with one at least of the causes why English law has failed in its beneficial effects, why it is so often a mere dead letter, and always an object of hatred and contempt; why, when executed, it is feared rather than respected; and why in so many cases whole classes of the people have been found to regulate their conduct, and to draw their opinion of right and wrong, not from the spirit of the laws which ostensibly rule them, but from that of secret codes of their own fabrication, according to which punishments are dealt out on principles in conflict with those recognised by the State, sanctioned by the irregular sallies of illegal violence, and all the other necessary attendants upon the decrees of secret associations entered into for the purpose of evading legal authority, or setting it at defiance.

Such a picture will not appear over-coloured if we examine the records of justice in Ireland, and find that by far the greater number of legal condemnations and penalties have been the punishment of crimes proceeding directly or indirectly from the action of secret associations of the kind.

The laws of England, it would seem then, have never been assimilated to the habits and temper of the people of Ireland. Was it that they were either in themselves ill-suited to the state of civilization of the country at the time they were introduced, or else that circumstances connected with its political history rendered their proper application impracticable?

Something may be attributable to each of these causes.

It is to be borne in mind, that the laws of England, as well as the methods of administering them, were things of slow growth.

It is one of the distinguishing qualities of the English law, as well as one of its boasts, that it is based upon "immemorial usage" rather than upon written statutes. The definition of the common or unwritten law, which is its foundation, implies that it has no other authority than tradition. "The memory of man runneth not to the contrary," is the expression used to describe its sanction; and not that it is to be found inscribed in any code drawn up at a stated time, or by a particular legislator, as is the case in regard to the Roman law, so generally adopted in Europe. Whatever may be the anomalies to be found in a body of laws thus gradually formed, it has been remarked with truth, that it is usually better fitted *to the country of its birth* than would be a code apparently more perfect in its parts, and more symmetrical in its arrangement.

Now even at the time English law was first introduced into Ireland, it would be difficult to imagine any system of jurisprudence more totally opposed than it was, in letter and in spirit, to the laws (if such they can be called) which existed amongst—but scarcely ruled—the barbarous and hostile tribes which occupied, or rather fought amongst themselves for the soil.

It is related of the Irish, at the time that Henry II. came to Ireland and effected what has erroneously been styled the conquest of the country, (for no such conquest *then* took place) that—

" All came in peaceably, and had large CONCESSIONS made them of the like laws and liberties with the people of England, which they gladly accepted."*

If it is true that the Irish chiefs accepted of this *boon*, and afterwards, as is averred, swore to King Henry that they would henceforth be governed by the laws of England, we apprehend that either they considered this engagement as a mere piece of courtesy to the English prince, on his leaving the country, after his peaceful visit, or else that they entered into it not knowing what they did. The amalgamation of English law and Irish custom was, in fact, a matter beyond their power, supposing it to have been agreeable to their inclination. What is certain is, that at any of the subsequent periods at which we get a glimpse of the troubled and obscure stream of Irish history, we find that no such amalgamation had actually taken place. Wherever (for many centuries afterwards) we find English *authority* existing in Ireland, it was both limited in extent to particular places, and was of a nature partaking more of the character of military occupation than of the establishment of law, while the rest of the country remained in the full exercise of its native barbarism.

The English conquest of Ireland was effected not by any single victory, or course of victories, by a British sovereign, nor yet by a general sub-

---

* Mollyneux's " Case of Ireland Stated," p. 13.

mission to his authority by the chieftains of the clans who occupied the island, but by the successive and isolated acts of invasion by military adventurers, acting, it is true, *feudally* as representatives of the King of England, but, in reality, each for himself, at his own expense, accompanied by his own vassals, and for his own profit or that of his followers. These expeditions had varied results, little attended to, and probably imperfectly known to the "Superior Lords" in England in whose name they were made. The history of these conquests is obscure, but such of the circumstances as are known of them, particularly that conducted by Strongbow, Earl of Pembroke, are sufficient to mark their true character. They bear greater analogy to the conquests by which Fernando Cortes and Pizarro added vast but unknown kingdoms to the Spanish Crown, than to the political subjugations of one kingdom by another, which have occurred in the more central parts of Europe.*

The epochs at which Ireland was really reduced to apparent acquiescence to English rule, and

* Nowhere is the loose and fluctuating nature of feudal tenure more completely illustrated than in the history of English occupations and invasions of Ireland; and it is remarkable, that some of the adventurers who undertook them were not Englishmen by birth. They may, in fact, be regarded as speculators, who went to seek their fortune in unknown lands, their capital being a certain amount of military skill and daring acquired in other wars.

abandonment of its own usages, were such as were unfavourable to any real assimilation of the English law to Irish uses; and we believe it is not too much to assert, that till the present hour no thorough assimilation has taken place.

There is another peculiarity of the English law to which we have adverted in the introductory part of these notes, which was unfavourable to its just or efficient administration in Ireland; we mean the principle of self-government, according to which, that law is in a great measure administered by the people upon themselves. In a nation where the population is homogeneous in race and united in religion, or, at all events, not divided into factions strongly opposed to each other in these respects, nothing can be more conducive to liberty than such a system—nothing better fitted to inspire the confidence of the people in the justice of its own laws, and to insure a ready recognition of their authority. Where this is not the case, and when race has been set against race, and sect against sect, for ages, any attempt to administer justice on the above-named principle will not only fail, but be productive of consequences the very reverse of what were contemplated.

This would occur even when the conflicting parties should be nearly equal in numbers and otherwise on equal terms; but in cases where a predominant minority exercises a recognised ascendancy over the remainder, and where the administration of the laws is mainly in the hands of that minority, all the evil consequences will be enhanced.

Such was the condition of Ireland at the times (for it was not done at once) when English laws and usages were *really* introduced into this country. It was usually at the termination of some civil or religious struggle that this took place. It was when a party smaller in numbers, but superior in strength, had just established its supremacy by force, that the establishment of English Courts of Law and the English system of municipal and local tribunals took place; and it must be borne in mind that they were cotemporaneous with other "Acts of Settlement," as they are called, by which the conquering party acquired a property in the greater part of the land forfeited by the vanquished.

It is little to be wondered at, that laws introduced under such auspices, were looked upon as part and parcel of a system of spoliation rather than as safeguards against injustice. By the party in the ascendant they were, no doubt, considered to be instruments of Government, but by the conquered as engines of oppression. When it is recollected, too, that the more complete establishment of English law in Ireland was coincident with the establishment of Protestantism as the religion of the empire at large, making the profession of other creeds, and more particularly that of the Roman Catholics, punishable as a crime by law, and that consequently Roman Catholics were excluded from any part in its administration, it ought to excite no surprise, that, in Ireland, where the mass of the population held to that communion, English law, which thus became the very embodiment of Protestantism, should be regarded with aversion and distrust. But even long after the extreme rigour of the penal code had been relaxed, and the profession of the Roman Catholic religion was no longer an offence, the law made so marked a distinction between Roman Catholics and Protestants, by means of disabilities, that the former were still virtually excluded from the administration of justice. It was consequently administered *upon them* not by a sovereign exercising arbitrary sway, but (what was infinitely more galling) by that part of their fellow-subjects which they had been accustomed to regard as their hereditary enemies. As time wore on, it is true, a greater degree of toleration was conceded to Roman Catholics; restrictions were withdrawn, grievances redressed, until the crowning measure (or what was *at the time* considered to be so) of Emancipation in 1829 was carried. Roman Catholics were then, and have been since, not only admitted, but invited to take part in the administration of justice.

But the old mistrust remained, and still to a

great extent remains, although Roman Catholics have been promoted to the most eminent posts in the judiciary, although the municipalities and the magistracy are open to them, and are now, the former mainly, the latter to a considerable extent, composed of persons of that persuasion. The same " strong conception," however, still prevails among the people that the law is unfairly administered, that it is an oppressor and not a protector, that judges are partial, that the verdicts of juries depend upon the manner in which they have been "packed," that magistrates oppress the poor and favour the rich, and that the whole course of justice is hostile and corrupt. So deep is this conviction, and so long has it existed, that argument or evidence seems now to be powerless to shake it. Little else could indeed be expected.

"Non pudet," says Cicero, "ab animis consuetudine imbutis quaerere testimonium veritatis."

The gradual establishment of other habits and impressions by time and experience can alone have that effect. In the meantime, nothing tends more surely to obstruct the course of justice than the existence of a rooted antipathy to its ministers and a distrust of its decrees. The minds of the administrators of justice themselves, as well as of those to whom it is administered, are warped by the existence of such a feeling, and justice itself cannot but suffer in the struggle. The magistrate, under such impressions, is sure to regard the law rather as an arm for self-defence against violence, and a means of chastising rebellion, than as an instrument for dispensing justice between man and man, and maintaining public order by its calm and impartial enforcement; the governed see in it a contrivance for their political subjection by a hostile and dominant class.

Under such circumstances, it has availed little that the Superior Courts of Ireland have been presided over by judges not only upright and above suspicion of corruption or inhumanity, but, in general, eminently qualified for their high functions. The Irish Bench can boast of names second to none in the records of jurisprudence. Such men as Anthony Malone, Plunket, or Bushe would do honour to any judiciary body. Nor was the Irish Bar, of whom such men were the representatives, in any respect inferior in character or talents to that of any other European country.

But as the decision of a case was never believed in Ireland to depend so much upon the abilities of the judge as upon the temper or composition of the jury, it was principally in regard to this that distrust was felt.

We have here, again, a notable instance of the inapplicability of the English system of law to the circumstances of Ireland. Trial by jury—the "Palladium," as it is considered, of English liberty—the guarantee of impartiality, and of exemption from undue influences, becomes, in Ireland, the least reliable of all tests of truth or justice, and the subject of universal discord and discontent. Nor is it easy to see how it can ever be otherwise, so long as a country is divided into two hostile camps, by political and religious animosities.

It would be in vain to tell an Irish Roman Catholic that his cause had been righteously judged by a Protestant jury. An Irish Protestant would be equally incredulous as to the justice of a sentence given against him by a jury of Roman Catholics. Men ceased to pay any attention to the evidence upon which a conviction or an acquittal was pronounced. They looked to who tried the case; what was the supposed politics of the judge; how was the jury composed; what was the religion of the witnesses; and upon all these, violence and intimidation was to be exercised, if the result threatened to be unfavourable to their party.

We have but too lately had to deplore instances of such proceedings.

Unfortunately the state of the country has frequently rendered it impossible to avoid the commission of irregularities by the legal authorities themselves. That juries have been what is called "packed," there can be no doubt. The plea of self-defence from imminent and immediate danger is the only one that can be alleged in palliation of such a practice. But that plea can sometimes be reasonably urged. There have been occasions on which convictions for crimes openly committed were absolutely necessary for the preservation of the authority of the Government, while, at the same time, there existed a moral certainty on all hands, that their authors would be acquitted by any jury taken without careful selection from the panel. All the resources of the law officers of the Crown, consequently, were used to eliminate from the juries such individuals as they well knew would never consent to the conviction of a man of their own party or sect, and to secure the presence of those who might be expected to be less biassed. This, no doubt, in some degree, deserves the name of "packing;" but whether it does or not, it most assuredly confirmed the public belief that such was the usual and approved practice of the law authorities in all such cases.*

It was, consequently, in respect to those parts of the administration of justice which most partook of the nature of that kind of self-government to which we have alluded that distrust was most felt. The composition of the juries, and the conduct of the officers upon whom their appointment depended, were ever the objects of incurable suspicion; and the jurisdiction of the magistracy

* See Evidence given before the House of Lords Committee on Crime, 1839.

was felt, or at all events believed to be, oppressive, and tainted with systematic partiality.

These leading features in the administration of justice in England—there justly regarded as most favourable to liberty—thus became in Ireland the most prominent subjects of jealousy and distrust. So evident was the existence of this feeling at the time from which we date our investigation, (1825,) that we find the attention of the Legislature was then directed to the subject.

It will now be our object to detail the measures which have been since taken, with a view of inquiring into and remedying such defects as might be found really to exist in the practical administration of justice in Ireland.

With respect, then, to the composition of juries, and to the conduct of the officers who conducted their appointment, we find that a Committee of the House of Commons, which had been appointed to inquire into the truth of allegations made against them, report as follows :—

" Opinions having gone abroad that justice was not impartially dispensed through the medium of juries in Ireland, and tending to render a large portion of the community dissatisfied with the administration of justice in this respect ; and it having been insinuated that persons professing the Roman Catholic religion, though otherwise qualified to serve as jurors, were intentionally excluded by the sheriffs, it was desirable to ascertain whether or not such information was founded on fact. With this view, the sub-sheriffs of counties at large have been examined, and their evidence satisfactorily proves the rumour to be destitute of foundation—save in a single county, in which it appears that it had formerly been the practice to exclude Roman Catholics from all panels, except that of the Grand Jury at Assize, but which exclusion has ceased in practice within the last year."

The conduct of the sub-sheriffs, upon whom the selection of juries practically devolves, having been at the same time complained of, was also made the subject of special inquiry, when the Commissioners reported :—

" With respect to juries in general, whatever grounds of complaint may formerly have existed against sub-sheriffs of counties as to the manner in which the panels are returned, we have no data before us to induce a belief that, in the exercise of this branch of duty, incorrectness has prevailed in the counties at large of later years. Loose and general complaints by individuals against whom verdicts have been given, and imputations cast by them upon the juries who have pronounced such verdicts, charging them with partiality and corruption, are sometimes heard; but these accusations, so far as the sub-sheriff is involved in the imputation, if they have any foundation in reality, have not, in any instance occurring in the counties at large, reached us in the form of actual proof."*

These statements are, no doubt, worthy of credit; but giving them their full weight, and supposing, consequently, that the want of confidence felt by the mass of the people in regard to the composition and the decisions of juries, to be in a great measure groundless, it continued to be, nevertheless, an incontestable fact that such want of confidence subsisted, and would do so as long as the political and religious animosities which have never ceased to prevail in the country existed. Even taking for granted that the juries were not unfairly chosen, and that their verdicts were not substantially unjust, a general belief that they were so, would be sufficient to deprive the institution of the greater part of its beneficial effect.

It appears to us, however, to be no exaggeration to affirm, that, allowing the purity on the part of law officers, sheriffs, and sub-sheriffs to have been unexceptionable, and the checks upon a partial selection of jurors the most ingenious that could be devised, no effectual means could ever be found in a country so politically situated as Ireland, for arriving at the nomination in every instance of juries whose composition could be unobjectionable to *both* of the parties into which the

* See Reports of Legal Inquiry Commissioners of 1824-1825.

nation is divided. Objectionable they always would be in cases where the political feelings of those parties were involved; and such cases have been (as we shall show when we come to treat of the peculiar characteristics of crime in Ireland) the great majority of those brought under the consideration of the courts of justice.

One of the consequences of this feeling of distrust was, moreover, peculiarly unfavourable to the impartiality of jurors; for systematic intimidation was exercised against them, as well as against the witnesses, by the friends of the criminals they convicted; and they were exposed to public obloquy, on the supposition of their having taken part in proceedings looked upon as oppressive or unjust, by the very class to which they themselves belonged.

With the design of removing some of the grounds for complaint, it was determined to render the selection of jurors as little dependent as possible upon the caprice or party bias of the High Sheriff. A bill was accordingly passed in the year 1833, (3 & 4 William IV., cap. 91,) which altered and clearly defined the qualifications for jurors, and which necessitated the names of the possessors of them being enrolled in the jury book from which juries must be struck. The effect of this measure was to increase the number of jurors, the majority of whom, however, were of a lower class, and less educated than those who formerly served.* But this measure, although placing persons on the panel totally irrespective of their religious creed, was of little avail in removing the distrust which existed, and its effect was to a great extent neutralized by the practice called " challenging," or the setting aside of a juror, as an unfit person to try the case. The prisoner was limited in his challenges; the Crown was unlimited: and as this unlimited right was occasionally exercised to an apparently excessive degree, its effect on the administration of the law was highly injurious, strengthening in the minds of the people the feeling that a person put on his trial was foredoomed, rendering the law, if possible, more unpopular, and increasing the reluctance to give evidence.

About the year 1835, this system was almost entirely abandoned by the Crown, and although such a course led often to the acquittal of undoubted offenders, yet the change tended, in some small degree, to lessen the antipathy exhibited by the great body of the people to the law.

To proceed to the consideration of that part of the administration of justice which devolves upon the magistracy, we may, in the first instance,

* Instances are given of men being placed on juries who were unable either to read or write; also, ribbonmen sat as jurors sometimes. See Q. 2523-4, Committee on Crime in Ireland, 1839.

direct our attention to the improvements which have been effected in the constitution and practice of the Courts of Quarter Sessions.

These Courts, which rank next to Courts of Judges of Assize, were, as originally established in Ireland, an assembly of two or more magistrates, on a day and at a place appointed, in order to hear and determine in regard to matters within the scope of their commissions. The magistrates who formed these Courts having been found deficient in the necessary knowledge of the law, and little disposed to study it, it became necessary to give them some aid and direction in the discharge of their duties. Accordingly it was enacted, (27th Geo. III., cap. 40,) that a barrister of six years' standing should be appointed to act as a constant "assistant" to the justices composing the Court. This system was extended to the whole of Ireland in 1796, and was everywhere in operation in 1825. By these Courts, felonies, petty larcenies, and misdemeanours, were cognizable. The sessions were held every three months, in several of the principal towns of each county, and were presided over by the "assistant barrister" as Chairman.*

There can be no doubt that the appointment of this officer was a considerable improvement in the constitution of these Courts.

* Legal Inquiry Commissioners' Reports.

Another improvement in that part of the administration of justice was made, or at all events attempted, by the general introduction of what are called "Petty Sessions," held by the local magistracy.

The enforcement of that part of law which, according to the English system, devolves upon justices of the peace, who are in daily and immediate contact with the peasantry, could not, in a country so politically situated as Ireland, but be a matter of extreme delicacy. To be successful, an amount of discretion, impartiality, diligence, and knowledge of the law, would be required, which was far from characterizing the Irish County Magistracy. Honourable exceptions could, no doubt, be adduced, but, as a class, it cannot be denied that it was deplorably deficient in all these qualifications. It was in general ill-composed—attorneys, middlemen, and persons who had perhaps formerly possessed landed property, but who had either lost it or were involved in debt, being admitted to perform functions, for the proper discharge of which personal respectability and independent circumstances ought ever to be indispensable conditions. The practice of absenteeism greatly aggravated the evil; but it is not unnatural that a magistracy so composed and so situated should not only have failed in producing the beneficial result for which it was intended, but should afford a constant subject of discontent, and confirm the habitual distrust of the people in the laws under which they were called upon to live.

So glaring, in fact, were the malpractices and defects of some of the magistracy, that a revision of it was attempted by the Government in the year 1823, when, in two counties in the south of Ireland, from twelve to twenty magistrates in each were removed from the Commission of the Peace for malversation or unfitness.*

It is clear that such a measure served rather to point out the existence of the evil than to cure it; the absence of proper materials for the formation of a magistracy of a better kind being the real cause of its inefficiency.

The practices, in fact, which had obtained in the administration of justice by magistrates in Ireland, were such as offered little guarantee against partiality or corruption, while they obviously favoured negligence and inefficiency; and it was in order to correct them in some measure that the institution of Petty Sessions was had recourse to.

Before the introduction of these sessions, magistrates were in the habit of exercising their functions without the check of publicity—they adjudicated cases at their private residences, and at such times as they themselves might choose to appoint.

* See evidence given before the Committee on the State of Ireland, 1824-5.

A single magistrate might thus either determine a case at what time or in what manner he might deem convenient; or he might neglect it altogether, or delay it indefinitely, if so disposed, without its being possible for the parties interested to exercise any effective control upon him in these respects, or to obtain any assurance, other than that of the individual character of the magistrate, of the impartiality of his proceedings.

By the Act 7 and 8 Geo. IV., cap. 67, Petty Sessions (which had already been adopted partially in Ireland) were established throughout the entire country.

" Whereas," says the Act, " the holding of Petty Sessions by Justices of the Peace in Ireland has been found conducive to a better administration of the laws, and to the general interests of His Majesty's subjects within that part of the United Kingdom; and whereas it is expedient to give additional facilities for holding such Petty Sessions, and for securing a uniform and effectual mode of procedure therein, be it enacted," &c., &c.

And it was enacted that at the next Quarter Sessions it should be lawful for the Justices of the Peace to divide the several counties into such districts as should seem to them most expedient for the purposes of the Act, and to fix a place for the holding of Petty Sessions. A record was to be kept of all the acts, orders, or proceedings done at Petty Sessions, and was to be signed by all the

Magistrates present, and from their decisions an appeal could be made to the superior Court of Quarter Sessions. All informations sworn at the Petty Sessions had to be transmitted to the Clerk of the Peace, or Crown, and every magisterial act at Petty Sessions had to be signed by two Justices at least.

The exercise of all magisterial functions by a single Justice of the Peace was thus submitted to vigilant supervision, and the publicity of the proceedings was in a great degree a guarantee against the exercise of partiality. Established in every district of the country, Petty Sessions gave a ready and accessible means of redress, of which the people were not slow to avail themselves in minor cases, whilst the frequent and regular meetings of Magistrates kept the law before them, and impressed them to some extent with the notion that justice was obtainable when they stood in need of it.

In requiring the presence of two Justices of the Peace to give validity to all acts at Petty Sessions, the state of extensive districts of Ireland had been overlooked, for in many places the resident gentry was not large enough to furnish a sufficient number of persons to act as Magistrates. Partly from this circumstance, partly from the fact that in many instances Magistrates, who were men of position and means, felt a disinclination to taking any very active part in cases in which popular feeling ran high, such as faction fights, organised outrages, or party processions, fearing that by so doing they would render themselves obnoxious to the people, and place their properties and lives in danger, the Government found it necessary in several counties to appoint paid officers to execute the duties naturally devolving upon a Magistracy. The people themselves, too, were in many cases desirous of having the law administered by a person nominated by the Crown.

The advantages arising from the appointment of these stipendiary Magistrates was felt to be so great, that it was determined to establish them as an institution. Accordingly, an Act (6 and 7 William IV., cap. 13) was passed to that effect; and since that time, both in the administration of the law and in the preservation of the peace, these officers have rendered valuable service.

There is one more measure connected with the Magistracy of the country to which we must advert. There existed no direct mode of communication between the Government and the Magistracy. Nor was there in the separate counties a responsible person who, from his rank and character in society, might communicate upon its state with the Government. To supply this want, the English custom was introduced; and by an Act passed in 1831, (1 and 2 William IV., cap. 17,) the appointment of lieutenants of counties was authorized. A political head to each county was thus created; and Magistrates were henceforth appointed upon their recommendation, instead of, as formerly, upon the recommendation of irresponsible persons.

Another improvement of considerable importance as regards the notorious impunity with which crimes of a certain class were committed in Ireland, was effected by a change adopted by the Government in regard to the trial of criminal cases. It had been usual to leave the prosecution of even the gravest crimes to the injured parties, the Crown limiting its interference to cases distinctly connected with insurrectionary movements and political offences. This was a practice which in Ireland was necessarily attended with unsatisfactory results. There has always been felt in this country an extreme reluctance on the part of individuals to appear as prosecutors, or even as witnesses, in cases where party or political feeling could be supposed to have place; and it must be observed, that the number of cases in which such feelings are not either directly or *indirectly* involved is very small. Where there exists an habitual disposition to resist or evade the law, the position of a prosecutor is often invidious, if not dangerous, independent of the hardship and expense to which he conceives himself subjected in that character; while the intimidation and summary acts of vengeance to which witnesses in criminal cases are exposed on the part of the friends of those involved, is too well known not to render them unwilling to give testimony which might lead to conviction. From these causes such prosecutions were either not undertaken, or else failed through the poverty, fear, or neglect of the prosecutor. Injured parties preferred, if possible, to take the law into their own hands, and one outrage thus became the source of many others.

The necessity of a more effective system of prosecutions in criminal cases was, however, at length recognized, and the Crown lawyers gradually brought a much greater number of such cases to trial. A greater degree of efficiency in the administration of the law was in this respect attained, but the progress was slow; for it appears from the report of the Committee of 1832, that even the Crown prosecutions of criminal cases still frequently failed, principally from the negligence and inefficiency of the Magistrates in the earlier stages of the proceedings.

A considerable improvement, too, was made in 1835, in the prosecution of offences at Quarter Sessions. Hitherto prosecutions at Quarter Sessions were not undertaken by the Crown, unless in very special cases, directed by the Attorney-General; but from this time many prosecutions were conducted by the Solicitors appointed for the purpose, called Sessional Crown Solicitors. The appointment of these officers has secured the effective prosecution of a very large class of cases, chiefly assaults, arising out of riots at fairs and other places, which were formerly prosecuted by the parties themselves, or, which was more frequently the case, compromised before trial, and not brought to justice at all.

These reforms, although well-intended and calculated to ameliorate the administration of justice, would, however, have proved inoperative in the absence of an effective public force, by which decisions obtained by better constituted tribunals, or improved legal proceedings, could be carried into effect.

That the want of any such efficient force had from the earliest times been felt is too notorious to be insisted upon, and it may be worth while to follow the steps which have been taken by the Government to provide it.

The first force of this kind was created in the year 1787, (27 Geo. III., cap. 40,) but it was soon found to be of little use in any way, and, especially, to be totally inadequate for the suppression of disturbances.

Accordingly, for this special object, a second force was organized in 1814, (54 Geo. IV., cap. 131,) called the Peace Preservation Police. When a district became disturbed, the Lord Lieutenant in Privy Council was empowered to proclaim it as being so, and in consequence to direct the establishment there of an extraordinary body of Police, the expense of which was to be levied upon the district in which it was placed—a plan calculated not only to prevent the commission of other offences, but also to inflict a punishment. But this force was small, whilst the other was inefficient, and some further change became necessary. Accordingly, in the year 1822, an Act (3 Geo. IV., cap. 103) was passed, and the police of Ireland assumed a regular form. A better system for its regulation was introduced; four provincial inspectors were named, who, subject to the Government, had each complete control within their respective provinces; and sixteen constables, appointed by the magistrates, were allotted to each barony.

The Peace Preservation Police was not, however, altered; so that there were two distinct forces in existence.

But although the new force was a decided improvement on its predecessor, it nevertheless did not succeed in giving satisfaction, and there existed a want of that vigour, efficiency, and unity of action, which was absolutely necessary for asserting the authority of the Government.

Further alterations were therefore deemed requisite; and in 1836, an Act (6th and 7th Wm. IV., cap. 13) was passed, remodelling the entire system, and combining into one effective force the two that had hitherto existed. Instead of four provincial inspectors, one inspector-general was appointed, who was placed in immediate connection with the Government; and the power of appointing the constables was transferred from the magistracy to the Lord Lieutenant. Numerous changes were made in the internal regulations and discipline.

The effect of these arrangements was soon shown in the increased vigour and exertions of the constabulary; and there was thus placed in the hands of the Government a powerful and effectual means of enforcing obedience to the law. Nor was it long before such means were made active use of, and the best effects followed, both in the detection of crime and in the suppression of those open and flagrant breaches of the law which were constantly taking place. The force now consists of about 12,000 men, all highly disciplined, placed in parties of not less than four or five each, in stations dotted all over the country, so that the whole of it is under the immediate surveillance of the civil power, and the Executive Government has direct and reliable communication with every part of it.

Five-and-thirty years have elapsed since the organization of the present force, and the men of which it is composed have ever exhibited themselves devoted to their duty, and have performed it on many critical and dangerous occasions in a manner worthy of much praise; nor is it too much to say, that the great diminution which has taken place in several classes of offences in Ireland is attributable to the activity and efficiency of the Constabulary.*

It will thus be seen that although the administration of justice in Ireland is still imperfect, and its improvement beset with difficulties, important and solid reforms both in the administration and in the enforcement of the laws have been in reality effected. Up to the present day, however, deplorable incidents force themselves upon our attention, proving that the old spirit of distrust of the course of justice and defiance of the law still lives, and that the accustomed arms of outrage and intimidation are still had recourse to. If, in the presence of political excitement—while questions affecting the rights of property, which touch the foundations of social existence, are in agitation—or during periods of physical suffering, springing from causes out of the control of human laws, these improvements in the administration of justice and the proper application of self-government have not yet borne their expected fruits, and even seem, for the present,

---

* Up to 1847, the expense of the police was borne one-half by the counties, one-half by the Consolidated Fund. As a sort of compensation for the hardship inflicted on Ireland by the repeal of the Corn Laws, the *whole* expense was transferred to the Consolidated Fund. This transfer, had, however, been previously recommended on other grounds by the Devon Commission.

checked in their progress—there is no reason to despair of their ultimate effects.

We must recollect that the operation of all such reforms is necessarily slow, constituting, as it must, to be really valuable, not merely an improvement in the technical proceedings of legal tribunals, and a better enforcement of their decisions, but a change in the feelings and habits of thought of the people in regard to them.

NOTE.—In judging of the advance of social and legal improvements, which, like that of the hands of a clock, is not immediately perceptible, it is often instructive to compare the present state of such matters with that which existed at some former period (but which has probably been forgotten.) Improvements in the administration of justice in Ireland contemplated by the English Government, have not been confined to recent times; and it may interest our readers to compare those which we have now attempted to describe with some of those designed by one of the most enlightened and humane of English statesmen, Sir William Cecil, Secretary to Queen Elizabeth. Speaking of the intended establishment of a Presidency for the improvement of law and order in the Province of Munster, Sir William recommends, in a paper drawn up by him on the subject:—

" Also it shall be lawful for the President and Council, or any three of them, the President being one, in cases necessary, upon vehement suspicion and presumption of any great offence in any party committed against the Queen's Majesty, to put the same party to torture, as they shall think convenient." (Presidency of Munster, Feb. 1, 1566, Irish MSS., Rolls' House.)

Sir William, it is true, seems anxious to show the careful and paternal spirit in which his proposed improvements are conceived, for he immediately adds:

" The Lord President is to be careful to observe Divine Service, and to exhort others to observe it; and also to keep a preacher, who shall be allowed his diet in the household to whom the said President shall cause due reverence to be given in respect of his office, which he shall have for the service of God."

See Froude's History of the Reign of Queen Elizabeth, vol. ii. p. 386.

The despatches of Sir H. Sidney (when Lord Deputy) to Cecil, there quoted, are instructive as to the state of law and justice in Ireland at that time; and when we lament that their administration in our own is still below the level of English civilisation, we must bear in mind the depths from which it has arisen to attain even its present state.

CHAPTER VI.

CRIME.

INTIMATELY connected with the administration of justice is the distinctive nature of crime in Ireland.

Without some consideration of its peculiarities, it would be difficult to account fully for the defects to which we have adverted in the administration of justice, and impossible to devise the reforms which may be required to remedy them.

The elaborators of codes of criminal law are fond of reducing the endless variety of human crime into distinct categories, and of assigning appropriate punishments to each possible offence.

There is no great difficulty in doing this, and codes exist which embody the general principles of criminal ethics in such a manner as to defy any *theoretical* criticism of their exactness. It has, however, been the well-founded objection to such bodies of criminal law and rules of criminal proceeding, that when they come to be applied to states of society different from that in which they have had their birth, they are found in some way or other to be inadequate to their purpose. Many of their provisions become inapplicable or useless; while, on the other hand, combinations are found to arise, and practices to prevail, which they have failed to foresee, and consequently to provide for. The general provisions of such codes become rapidly encrusted with interpretations and exceptions, precedents and cases come to be cited as in customary law; and the boasted and, no doubt, desirable simplicity of the few articles under which every species and degree of crime have been classed, becomes obscured by the innumerable commentaries.

The fate of the Code Napoleon, the most complete, the clearest, and most admirable body of the sort in existence, will illustrate this position. The glosses and interpretations, the citation of decisions on doubtful points, the intricacies, the arguments on disputed principles, already afford ample food for the industry, learning, and acuteness of the French lawyers and judges, whose task in these respects, it might be supposed, would have been rendered easy by the lucid plainness and brevity of its text.

Where a system of criminal jurisprudence is transferred, so to say, in a block from one country to another, or even from one part of the same country to another, where different habits of crime subsist, something more than this inconvenient accumulation of legal commentary takes place.

In such cases the laws become either inoperative or injurious; or else, in order to adapt themselves to the new circumstances under which they are administered, they are distorted in spirit, misapplied in practice, forced aside from their original meaning, exacerbated in some respects, softened in others, strained in their interpretation, or fitfully aided by supplementary or temporary enactments, which strike at the very root and spirit of the principles on which the whole code was originally founded.

Crime, in almost every country, presents what may be termed a distinct physiognomy; and so long as the laws are not specially adapted to this, they remain comparatively inefficacious. Such differences were, no doubt, more striking in the middle ages and in the earlier centuries of modern history than in the present times, but they still exist.

A reference to some familiar instances in Great Britain itself, however, may illustrate our meaning. The laws as executed on the Scottish border, even in the reign of Elizabeth, and known by the name of "March Treason Pains"—by which cattle lifting, rick burning, private raids, &c., were summarily punished by death or mutilation, on the sole authority of the Lord Warden of the March—were certainly neither required nor enforced in the city of London, or in the county of Kent, even in those times; while the intricate litigation in regard to frauds, swindles, libels, illegal publications, treasonable practices, poisonings, and secret assassinations, the innumerable subjects of law in more civilized communities, were little wanted on the Scottish or Welsh Marches.

And so of Ireland. In no country has the physiognomy of crime been more strongly marked, or more peculiar. Accordingly, we find that in no part of the empire has the English system of law suffered greater distortion or anomalies in its application. In none have more partial abrogations on the one hand, and supplemental enactments on the other, been required to give it even the efficacy required for the bare self-defence of the authority and existence of the Government. Insurrection Acts, Acts against the administration of illegal oaths, against the possession of fire-arms, Acts suspending the Habeas Corpus, have all been necessary, and have all tended to the practical introduction of that absolutism, a guarded jealousy of which constitutes the distinctive spirit of English law. It consequently affords no matter for surprise, that such an antagonism between principle and practice should result in a system at once weak, vexatious, unequal, and oppressive.

It may be worth while, therefore, to examine some of the circumstances which have given their peculiar colour to the crimes which have been most prevalent in Ireland.

In the first place it will be remarked, that the great majority of the offences which it is the business of the law to suppress or punish, consist, and have ever consisted, in hostilities to the Government itself, or when in crimes against individuals, in acts of violence or intimidation exercised against them in connection with some predetermined system of resistance or evasion of the law. The number of crimes between man and man has in Ireland ever been a small proportion to those arising out of the relative position of a conquering to a conquered race, and to the animosities of opposed differing religious creeds.

We shall have little difficulty in accounting for this peculiarity, when we reflect that Ireland, although a conquered country, is one of which the subjugation was slowly, irregularly, and, perhaps, never thoroughly effected. A chronic state of resistance to the conquering element subsisted for ages, favoured sometimes by the weakness, often by the neglect or ignorance of the invading power, but more than anything by the disorders, dissensions, and corruption of the English settlers themselves, who succeeded in partially occupying the country. The civilizing process which might have been expected from the infusion of a comparatively advanced race into a semi-barbarous population, was painfully gradual, subject to disastrous refluxes, and ultimately imperfect.

We have but to refer to the reports of the Lords Deputies during the reign of Elizabeth to become aware that the state of the things within the English settlements, or what was called the Pale, was as bad and often worse than that without it.

All the atrocities incident upon the occupation of a half-conquered country by a force of undisciplined and ill-paid adventurers seem to have been rife within the districts which composed it; while such a force was inadequate to defend them from the incursions of the scarcely more barbarous but not more flagitious natives without.* The pathetic but unavailing appeals to his sovereign of the brave and loyal Sidney, when Deputy, either to be furnished with the means of maintaining order and enforcing justice, or to be relieved from the odious task of attempting to govern Ireland, affords more information in regard to the nature of the crimes then prevalent in Ireland, than could be gathered from the most elaborate historical disquisition.

Nor let it be objected, that it is irrelevant to refer to times so distant, for it was in those times that Irish crime assumed its distinctive character— a character by which, although we may be thank-

* See Froude's History of Elizabeth, vol. iii.

ful that it has been much mitigated, it is still indelibly marked.

It is evident that in a protracted war of this kind, which was waged between the settlers and the natives, all questions relating to the use and possession of the land must have had a prominent place; and the nature and conditions under which it was held, or rather used, by the native Irish tribes at the time of the English invasions, contributed to give a peculiar character to the struggle.

The state of the native Irish appears to have been in a great degree pastoral and nomadic, nor in this respect did it differ from that of other European countries at that period, although it was opposed to the system already prevalent in England. Among the native Irish but a small portion of the lands seems to have been appropriated, or enclosed, or held in farms by any fixed tenure; nor did the kind of agriculture by tillage, which necessitates a fixed local or individual proprietorship, prevail to any great extent. The rights exercised in regard to land were rather those obtained or assumed by the Irish tribes, of pasturage for their flocks in the districts they claimed to rule over, which were exercised loosely, and in common by the septs, the wealth of each individual depending more upon the number of head of cattle he possessed, than in any marked portion of land of which he was the sole proprietor. This is a state of things which, wherever it prevails, is for obvious reasons the source of eternal broils and dissensions between neighbouring tribes, and of just such petty wars as we know existed among the Irish. We find, indeed, in the wars carried on between them and the English invaders, even to later times, the evidence of this state of things as regards the proprietorship of land. The object of every expedition, whether in wars between Irish chieftains or between them and the English, seems to have been, not so much the possession of portions of cultivated territory, or even its devastation, but the driving off or destruction of the cattle belonging to the tribe against which it was undertaken. Forming, as this did, both the chief food and the chief wealth of the tribe, it was in proportion to the success obtained in this object that victory or failure in the contest depended.

The events of the war between Sussex and Shane O'Neill, and between that chief and Sidney, the latter of which has more resemblance to a combined military operation than any other in the history of Ireland in those times, fully illustrate this condition of things; the alternate success of each party seems to have been invariably decided by the degree of efficacy in this mode of warfare, and the ultimate defeat of O'Neill was evidently determined by it.*

See Froude's History of England—Reign of Elizabeth, vol. ii.

As the limits of the English Pale were extended, a different system came into operation. The lands annexed to it were enclosed, and appropriated either to some individual of the English invaders, or to some Irishman under their protection and in their alliance; the encroachments thus effected upon what the native Irishry considered to be their natural rights, being equally odious to them in either case. Thus, by a continuance of the ill fortune which seemed to preside over all Irish affairs, the only means by which the products of the country could be increased, or its civilization advanced, were rendered baleful to its native inhabitants, by being associated with what was felt by the natives, and with what no doubt frequently was, the invasion, tyranny, and oppression of the stranger.

It is evident that without the appropriation and enclosure of the lands, the comparative barbarism and poverty of Ireland must have continued to subsist.

Although the analogy is not perfect it is considerable between the relative condition of the native Irish in regard to the English settlers, and that which took place between the New England colonists and the North American tribes. A hunting ground of several hundred miles square was barely sufficient for the subsistence of a small number of Indians, warriors as they styled themselves, because even that precarious and scanty subsistence was only maintained at the expense of never-ceasing war with neighbouring tribes. As the white man advanced, levelling the forest, tilling the soil, and introducing civilization into the country, he could only maintain himself by force and by the violation of rights theoretically superior to his own. The Indian claimed the land as his country; and it may be said, without much exaggeration, that it was to the superiority of the rifle to the tomahawk, and of civilized intelligence to savage cunning, that the title of the English colonists, now so widely developed in those lands, was founded. The Indian race was driven off to other deserts, or, more frequently, was exterminated. We have, consequently, heard less of its wrongs than of those of the Irishry, although in kind they were by no means dissimilar.

The reduction of the land in Ireland to regular proprietorship was slow, fitful, and dependent upon the gradual conquest of the country, which, as we have already observed, was ever imperfect. We find, consequently, that even in comparatively recent times, the extent of land in a state of commonage was still very great, and that whenever a further enclosure and appropriation of the land so left was attempted, it was met with resentment and resistance.

About the year 1740, the farmers of Munster attempted to enclose a considerable extent of commons upon which the tenants had a right of feeding. By this process, the poorer tenants were either ejected or called upon to pay a high rent, by the persons to whom the newly-enclosed lands were let, then called " land pirates," and since better known by the name of " middlemen." Secret associations were formed, then known by the term, " Levellers"—descriptive enough of their own immediate object, which was to tear down enclosures, destroy new-made roads, and place other impediments in the way of the practice to which they objected. Their operations, at first confined to such objects, were, however, soon directed to other grievances respecting the tenure of land. The tithes were a tax on land more peculiarly odious, as being levied for the support of a religion opposed to their own. The secret societies which set themselves to reform this grievance, obtained the well-known name of Whiteboys, from the disguise of white shirts under which they perpetrated their nocturnal outrages. There were many other denominations for similar purposes, among which were those called the " Carders," from a hideous kind of torture which they inflicted upon their victims, by stripping them naked and lacerating their bodies with a wool-card; " Oak Boys," " Heart-of-Steel Boys," were all scions of the same stock, whose vengeance was directed against certain "corvées," such as the six days' work, or other grievances, real or imaginary, inflicted by the agents of absentee proprietors. The pseudonym under which the greater part of the threatening notices and announcements of vengeance were made was that of "Captain Rock," a name which soon became a mythical incarnation of the spirit of agrarian outrage.

Even in cases where northern Protestants were concerned, and where it might be doubted whether the hands of "Captain Rock" could be traced, Moore, in his assumed autobiographical history of the rise and progress of this personage remarks:—

"The Rocks are no bigots in *fighting* matters, nor, indeed, at all particular as to whom they fight *with*, so it be *against* the common enemy, *i.e.*, generally speaking, the constituted authorities for the time being." "The English Government," he adds, "has at all times consulted our taste in this particular, ministering to our love of riot through every successive reign, from the invasion of Henry II. down to the present day, so as to leave scarcely an interval during the whole 600 years in which the Captain Rock for the time might not exclaim—

'Quæ regio in terris nostri non plena laboris!'

Or, as it has been translated by one of my family:—

'Through Leinster, Ulster, Connaught, Munster,
Rock's the boy to make the fun stir!'"

The Whiteboys were temporarily suppressed,

not through the ordinary action of the law, but by military force.

But the spirit of insurrection was far from being eradicated, and the peasantry immediately entered into a new combination, calling themselves "Right Boys," and resembling their predecessors in everything but name. The obnoxious impost of tithe became more immediately the object of their hostility; but they procceded also to regulate the price of land, to raise the price of labour, and to oppose the collection of taxes. They bound themselves by a secret oath to resist the laws of the land, and to obey none but those of "Captain Right;" whilst in all their proceedings they acted with a degree of caution and circumspection which was the more alarming, as it demonstrated system and design.

For their suppression the ordinary powers of the law were found insufficient. Further extraordinary provisions became necessary, and an Act was accordingly passed in 1787, "to prevent tumultuous risings and assemblies, and for the more effectual punishment of persons guilty of outrage, riot, and illegal combinations, and of administering and taking unlawful oaths."

At this time it was that the necessity of having some permanent civil force became recognised, and the first armed police force was created.

Whilst the "Right Boys" were carrying on their illegal proceedings in the South of Ireland, another and more formidable combination was entered into in the North, called "the Defenders," a name which they adopted from their combining to defend themselves against the domiciliary visits of their Protestant neighbours, called the "Peep-o'-Day Boys," who, fearing that the Catholics were collecting arms, wished to disarm them.

Although possessing this name, however, they did not the less act on the *offensive*, or confine themselves to those counties where the "Peep-o'-Day Boys" existed, and the system rapidly spread throughout the country. As their strength increased, their objects became more political, and they adopted offensive measures against the Government, who protected their enemies—a term which included all that possessed property and character. In every place, they committed the most barbarous outrages, compelling landlords to reduce their rents, refusing the payment of tithes, threatening the extermination of their opposers, and engaging in such desperate encounters occasionally that, on one occasion, they lost forty-eight men.

To check this spirit of turbulence, and to strengthen the arm of the civil power, some volunteer corps were raised, and the most strenuous efforts were made to render some of the offenders amenable to justice—efforts which were so far successful, that at one assizes in Louth, in 1793, twenty-one Defenders were sentenced to death, and thirty-seven to transportation and different terms of imprisonment.

Whilst the Defenders were in the full exercise of their power, a society was formed in 1791, called the "Society of United Irishmen," which, although in the first years of its existence aimed only at Parliamentary Reform, and the total abolition of the Penal Code, yet, as popular discontent and disturbance increased throughout the kingdom, gradually changed its object—first to "a national legislature," and ultimately to revolution and the establishment of a republican government —its language became more violent, its proceedings more daring, and the original test of membership was changed into an oath of secrecy.

In the year 1796, a coalition took place between this society and the Defenders, the name of United Irishmen being preserved. The Defenders, although numerous and active in almost every county, had, in different places, something peculiar to themselves, and wanted that uniformity of aim which distinguished the system of the United Irishmen.

The organization now attained was very perfect, and is worth describing, as exhibiting one of the peculiar characteristics of Irish crime, for somewhat similar organizations have since then, on other occasions, been also adopted.

The inferior societies consisted of not more than thirty-six members, each of which chose a secretary. The secretaries of five societies formed what was called a lower baronial committee, which had the immediate superintendence and control over those below it. From each of these committees, one member was delegated to an upper baronial committee, who in their turn sent each a member to the district committee. The several counties and towns being thus organized, a subordinate directory was established in each of the four provinces, and a general executive committee, composed of five persons, was elected by the provincial directories. In all these proceedings the greatest secrecy was observed, and every device used that was calculated to baffle detection.

When the determination to obtain the objects of the association by open force of arms was come to, a military organization was engrafted on the civil, the members were exhorted to obtain arms and ammunition, which they did so effectually, that by the end of the year 1796, the number of armed men had reached 500,000. Aid was also sought from Republican France.

For such a conspiracy, even in its commencement, the ordinary powers of the common laws of the country were totally inadequate, and the means of enforcing them entirely insufficient. To strengthen the Executive Government, therefore, the loyal subjects were enrolled into yeomanry corps, the Habeas Corpus Act was suspended, and an Act, entitled the "Insurrection Act," was passed in 1796, to prevent unlawful assemblies, and authorizing the Lord Lieutenant to "proclaim" any county where disturbances existed, whereupon every person residing in such counties were obliged to keep within their dwellings between sunset and sunrise, and if found offending against it, the magistrates were empowered to send such persons on board his Majesty's navy.*

The extraordinary powers thus conferred were of great assistance in grappling with the disturbers; but the insurrection nevertheless broke out—the civil law was superseded, and martial law substituted, and drum-head courts-martial took the place of trial by jury. The events which then followed were the suppression of a rebellion by military force, and the extinction of the Society of United Irishmen—

"Which," says Dr. Madden, in his well-known work on United Irishmen, "whether viewed in the character of its members, or the nature of its proceedings, may certainly be regarded as a confederacy which no political or revolutionary

* This Act further provided that the information of any prosecutors on behalf of the Crown, who might be assassinated, should be admitted as evidence against delinquents. Any person having arms was required by it to register his name and place of abode, and a magistrate might search the house of any person who should not do so. If a magistrate or peace-officer was murdered while on duty, or in consequence of his exertions to serve the public, the Grand Jury might levy a sum of money on the county for his representative.

society, that has gone before it, has surpassed in importance, boldness of design, and devotion to its principles, however mistaken they may have been."

For some years after the suppression of this rebellion, the country was so agitated and unsettled, that the Habeas Corpus Act remained suspended, and martial law was continued.

Nor was it long before another secret society pressed itself into notoriety, under the name of the "Threshers;" and according to long established custom their threatening letters and notices were signed by a mythical "Capt. Thresher." They assumed this name from the practice of threshing the tithe-proctor's corn, and rendering it valueless; but they did not confine themselves to this, and outrages similar to those perpetrated by the Whiteboys were committed by them. They assumed, indeed, even the same dress as their ancestors the Whiteboys, and for some time held the position of that notorious body.

Other illegal bodies, styling themselves "Shanavests" and "Caravats," were also formed, and the members pursued the already well-trodden path of regulating rents and tithes, and enforced their regulations by visiting and punishing those who disobeyed them.

These bodies were suppressed only by means of the military, and by the immediate administration of the law (upon such offenders as were caught) through means of Special Commissions, the Judges of which could often only move through the country with a large escort of troops.

But no sooner had one county been tranquillized by these means, and one illegal society suppressed, than another county became disturbed, and another society sprang into existence. And in the meantime, the Government had to be armed with the extraordinary powers of the Insurrection Act and the Arms Act; but even these provided only imperfectly for the suppression of offences committed by the members of these secret societies, and were never adequate for their prevention.

Independent of agrarian crime such as we have been describing, there was another description of disturbance peculiar to the Irish, and one to which they were much addicted. This was the "faction fight." No political association is implied in this term. Factions were but the remnant of the old system of clanship, the spirit of which still prevailed to a great extent in Ireland. They were composed of families and connections; and although in some parts of the country where there was a mixed population of Protestants and Roman Catholics, religion had a great effect in dividing them, still in other parts, where the population was entirely Roman Catholic, factions were as numerous, and faction fights as bitter.

The fights generally arose at a fair or some such

public meeting, where some of the peasantry got intoxicated. A quarrel ensued; one party prepared his friends or faction to meet the other on the next convenient occasion, and desperate fights ensued. Armed with rude but formidable weapons, lives were often taken, and persons maimed for life. The beaten faction then recruited for the next meeting place, until at last almost the whole peasantry were engaged, several hundreds being often seen on each side.

Such contests produced on the minds of the lower orders the most mischievous notions of their own power. They acquired a kind of discipline; they became habituated to acts of atrocious cruelty; they obtained leaders; and as these were generally chosen on account of personal strength or courage, there was an emulation, which tended to aggravate the nature of the fights. With these *open* breaches of the law, however, the Government was able to grapple, and they were ultimately successfully suppressed.*

When the great war with France came to a conclusion in 1815, and when the new policy of consolidation began to be pursued, the interest of the land-owners and of the tenants became, if possible, more than ever opposed to each other. On the one hand, the peasant seeking to retain pos-

---

* See Drummond's evidence before the Committee on Crime, 1839.

session of the plot of ground which afforded him almost the sole means of subsistence ; on the other, the land-owner seeking to regain control over his property, and to check the evil of an ever-increasing population, which was fast leading to anarchy and ruin. The enforcement of these opposing interests resulted in nothing less than a social war.*

The better to effect their purposes, the peasantry entered into fresh and more powerful combinations, which were formed upon the old model of the Whiteboy system, and improved by experience. Their object, perhaps more than formerly, was directed to such measures as would enable the tenant to retain possession of the land. The most daring outrages were perpetrated with this view, and as the landlord or his agent were not always assailable, and violence against them had not always the desired result, the popular vengeance was directed against the individual who was bold enough to take and cultivate a farm, or even a *part* of it, from which another had been ejected.

About this time, there rose into existence another of those numerous secret societies, which form so striking and peculiar a feature in the history of Irish crime—more efficiently organised than any which had gone before it, more unfailing in the execution of its judgments, and more dan-

---

* See evidence given before the Committees on the State of Ireland, 1824 and 1825.

gerous than any, if we except that of the United Irishmen. This was the Riband Society. Its exact origin is unknown; its objects, except so far as could be gathered from seeing its punishments, have never been exactly ascertained. All the information that has been obtained concerning it has necessarily been from men of the most infamous character, on whose testimony no reliance could be placed, except when it has been corroborated by circumstantial evidence.

The details of its organization are, however, partially known.*

It appears from general testimony, that the members were sworn to secrecy, to mutual support, and, under the penalty of death, to obedience to their leader, no matter what his commands might be. Each local society appeared also to have its officers, the principal of which was called the parish master; but great obscurity exists as to how far these local societies were connected together, and as to whether they were united under one common directory or head. It has been stated that there were district masters and county delegates, but the members in general appear never to have been aware of any leaders of note, although declaring that they were acting under some authority; and as even a surmise at

* See Evidence, House of Lord's Committee on Crime, 1839; and Evidence, House of Commons' Select Committee on Crime, 1852.

their names has never been obtained, the probability seems to be that there has never been a single head, but that the separate societies have acted independently of each other, their community of aim blending them all into one general association.

This aim, like that of all the other illegal societies, has been the regulation of dealings in land; but it has passed beyond this, and extended itself to the relations of employer and labourer— of master and servant. A political object, too, it must be said to have, insomuch as its principles, if carried successfully to their full extension, would amount to revolution.

Nor let it be thought that because in some districts the organization of Ribandism is almost unknown, the system is the less a reality. The spirit which is the foundation of all such societies does exist throughout almost the entire country.

With the growth of the system of consolidadation, crime increased; every fresh series of evictions or clearances seeming to rouse into renewed action the hostility of the peasantry.* With the increasing population, the demand for land became greater, and the difficulty of obtaining subsistence in other ways increased.

With unflagging zeal the peasantry acted upon

* See evidence given before the Committees of 1824-5, 1830, 1832. Also the evidence given before Land Occupation Commissioners, in 1845.

the code which they themselves had framed. And it was vain to expect that any moral feeling or regard for human life would deter them from carrying out its provisions.

To illustrate the desperate measures to which they sometimes resorted, we give the following short account of the proceedings in the case of the Ballinamuck estate of Lord Lorton.*

The property was in a state of great impoverishment. It had been divided and sub-divided over and over again, till it was covered by a description of people perfectly incapable of holding ground, scarcely one of them being able to stock his holding. When the lease fell in, it became necessary to do something for their relief, and for the improvement of the property. The tenants were accordingly turned out, under an arrangement which in every point of view was most liberal, receiving as a voluntary gift sums varying from £21 to £1 10s., in addition to a remission of the arrears of rent. Nine Protestant tenants were introduced on the estate.

The first was murdered close to his own house, the second was attacked and disabled for life, the third had his cattle destroyed, the fourth was stabbed, the fifth was *three* times fired at and ultimately shot dead; the houses of the sixth and

* See Lord Lorton's evidence before the Committee of the House of Lords on Crime, 1839.

seventh were attacked, and their cattle killed; the eighth was murdered in the presence of his family, and the ninth in the centre of a village. Thus, out of nine persons, four were murdered, two desperately wounded, and the property of the remaining three destroyed. No convictions were had in any of these cases.

To the time of the famine in 1846, agrarian crime continued with unabated though varying vigour ;* but that event, by effecting a reduction in the population, and by lessening the competition for land, weakened some of the stimulants to crime hitherto existing. The old spirit, however, remained; and though at times apparently dormant, it ever and again breaks out into fresh violence, giving evidence of its vitality and unimpaired vigour.

All the improvements in the administration of justice, including the creation of a special force of admitted efficacy, have hitherto but very imperfectly provided for the prevention of crime in Ireland; and although some of those offences which are common to most countries have been

---

* In 1826, there were 547 *committals* for murder and manslaughter.
„ 1829, „ 539 „ „ „
„ 1832, „ 620 „ „ „
„ 1837, „ 712 „ „ „
the larger proportion of which were agrarian. See Crime Committee, 1839.

considerably reduced, yet those which give to Irish crime its distinctive features have been but little affected.*

The peculiar kind of moral "virus" which had penetrated and pervaded all the relations of Irish life connected with the land tenure, cannot be better painted in a few brief sentences than are to be found in the following extracts from the charges of two of the Irish Judges. Men, both of them, eminently qualified by their talents and experience to appreciate and point out its malignant nature and influence—Chief Baron Smith and Chief Justice Bushe. The former in a charge to

---

* We select the following interesting and instructive evidence from that taken before the Select Committee of the House of Commons on Outrages in Ireland, at the comparatively recent date of 1852. The gentleman who gives it, (a stipendiary magistrate) had been for twenty-seven years in the public service in Ireland.

" You have," said one of the Committee, who was examining him, " all the appliances of the Government at your command, the police, the military, and every force the law can afford you— have you not?"

" Yes; in the fullest way I can desire."

" You are resident in the district ?"

" Yes, I am."

" And yet these ten or twelve prime movers (in the disturbance of the district) baffle all your efforts?"

" Yes; so far."

" They are stronger than you, stronger than the law, and all the appliances of the Government ?"

" Yes; they have such cunning, and their plans are so well devised, and carried out, that they baffle all."

the Grand Jury of the Queen's County, in 1832, says:—

"I perceive an anomalous and most pernicious union of anarchy with rule. I may not see who form the directory, and yet perceive that there is one. I hear sufficient ungracious speeches from their spurious thrones. I see edicts and proclamations, illegal notices and ejectments. I see an unlawful criminal code arraying itself against and attempting to supersede the legal one, surrounding itself with disorderly sanctions and seditious terrors, having its oaths and obligations; its ministers of injustice; its secret treasuries and supplies; its magazines of arms, collected by nightly plunder, seemingly to furnish its standing army of insurgent force. I see its capital punishments, its banishings, its maimings, its mulcts of property, its domiciliary visits, house-burnings, and attacks."

And the latter, at the Maryborough Special Commission, in 1832, says:—

"Whoever confines his estimate of such a confederacy to the mere outrages and crimes it produces has, I fear, but superficially examined the subject. Such consequences may be occasional and transient; but the moral influence upon society of such a diseased state of human character must be deep and permanent; the bad passions let loose, the charities of life extinct, those relations dissevered which, between the higher and the lower classes are the offspring of reciprocal protection and dependence, confidence displaced by suspicion, and fear and hatred in all classes vitiating and corroding the heart of man. These are productive seeds which threaten a fearful growth."

Sir George Cornwall Lewis has also well summed up the characteristics of Irish crime, although sometimes, as might be expected, in an English rather than an Irish point of view:—

"It pervades," says he, "the whole society. It is not the banding together of a few outcasts who betake themselves to illegal courses, and prey on the rest of the community, but it is the deliberate association of the peasantry. .... Its influence even when unseen is general; it is, in fact, the mould into which Irish society is cast—the expression of the wants and feelings of the great mass of the community." (Irish Disturbances, by Sir G. C. Lewis.)

Sir G. C. Lewis, in another place, correctly compares the immediate action of secret societies for agrarian purposes in Ireland to Trades Unions in England, and he is surprised to find that they "do not end or begin in religious animosities." But what he, in common with many English statesmen who have occupied themselves with the state of Ireland, passes over or underrates is, that all these societies had and have a general substratum and foundation in the intense and habitual disaffection of the whole of the lower and a great part of the middle classes of Ireland against the British Government, and their repugnance to the British connection, evinced more especially towards those classes which they conceive represent that connection *in Ireland*. In this is included, even when not expressed, religious animosity, because the above-named distinctions of origin and position are more or less accurately coincident with those of the two antagonistic creeds by which its whole population is divided. It is not unnatural that the statesmen who have carried on the Imperial Government, or that the English public, more particularly since what may be called the "period of concessions" began, should be slow or unwilling to perceive this, their theory being, that just in proportion as Irish grievances should be removed, Irish loyalty would grow up, and Irish disaffection wither. They were not prepared to acknowledge that the removal of habitual grievances, the relief from material burthens, the alleviation of distress, and the undoubtedly increased prosperity of the country, should, instead of having laid at rest for ever the spirit of rebellion, have rendered it more rampant and aggressive than before—more formidable, as having instilled itself into classes better able to organise it, supported and encouraged by another Ireland across the Atlantic, free and unshackled in the expression of its hostility, and impelled by a fanaticism not the less violent from being purely theoretical and sentimental on their own part, aiming at objects which it did not before openly affect—the more moderate section demanding a *virtual*, the more violent, if not more numerous party, an *actual* separation from the dominion of Great Britain.

The unfavourable result of the attempt to win the hearts of the Irish is slowly and unwillingly admitted, because it is contrary to the honest desires and confident predictions of the statesmen who have been labouring in so good a cause, and of the English people, whose good-will and sympathy with their Irish fellow-subjects have been long manifested in a thousand ways; but if other proof of this disheartening failure were wanting, the state and nature of Irish crime in reference to the administration of English justice would amply supply it.

CHAPTER VII.

ROMAN CATHOLIC EMANCIPATION.

THE most important measure respecting Ireland, since the Union, was the Roman Catholic Emancipation Act.

It is not our intention, nor is it necessary here, to chronicle the number of times it was discussed and rejected, to give a list of its supporters, or a history of the gradual change of opinion on the subject; suffice it to say, that the last time it came under the consideration of the Legislature it was brought forward in connection with two other subjects—

The first, the payment of the Roman Catholic Clergy by the State;

And the second, an increase of the qualification of the election franchise.

The first of these was soon found to be impracticable, and was abandoned. The second was the subject of a separate Bill — that for the disfranchisement of the forty shilling freeholders.

The disabilities under which the Roman Catholics laboured consisted in exclusion from both Houses of Parliament, and from almost all the important offices of the State and the Judiciary, namely — the Lord Lieutenancy of Ireland, the Chancellorship, and all other Judgeships, the offices of Attorney or Solicitor General, and the distinction of King's Counsel. They were ineligible to the Shrievalty and to many of the principal municipal corporation offices in Ireland. They were, in a word, excluded from all participation, and considered as unworthy of all trust, in carrying on the executive Government or the administration of justice of their country.

If these disabilities were imposed upon them under the presumption of their inherent and incurable hostility to the order of things established by the Revolution of 1688, it is on the other hand evident, that so long as such invidious distinctions should be maintained, their hostility could never be expected to die away, or much less to be replaced by a loyal concurrence in the general interest, glory, and prosperity of the Empire.

Somewhat inconsistently with this maxim of necessary distrust of Roman Catholic co-operation in any shape, in carrying on what was conceived to be an irrevocably established and exclusive Protestant Government, Roman Catholics, both English and Irish, were permitted to enter the army and the navy, to arrive at the highest ranks, to exercise the most important commands, and to receive the honorary distinctions attainable in those services, and thus to place themselves in positions where their disaffection to the sovereign or the State could, if it existed, manifest itself with the most destructive effect. Roman Catholics, besides this, enjoyed all civil rights, they could elect members to Parliament — although they themselves could not sit there—and they acted as magistrates and served as jurors.*

It will thus be seen, that at the period from which we date our investigation, a state of things existed in Ireland, the most fatal that can well be imagined to the functions of a representative and de-centralized Government such as that of Great Britain.

Under the influence of the religious ideas which prevailed in the States of Europe during the sixteenth and seventeenth centuries, an attempt had always been made by the predominant sect to ignore, if not to exterminate, every other. Successful in some instances, in Ireland it had failed.

The legal constitution of the State, which *assumed* the existence of religious unity, had in that country been always, and still continued to be, at variance with the fact—a variance which became every day more glaring as the vehemence of reli-

* Committee—State of Ireland, 1824-5.

gious intolerance gradually abated—and the notion that absolute identity of belief was an indispensable element in a national Government, though still entertained by many, began to lose ground. The evident want of success which had attended every effort to annihilate the religion of the majority of the Irish, and to force or induce them to adopt that of the State, produced at length some disposition to desist from so hopeless an enterprise; and the abolition of the penal laws may be taken as an indication that the expectation of reducing Ireland to religious obedience by the usual methods of persecution had been tacitly given up.

But the measure was imperfect, and, as is perhaps oftener the case in representative Governments than in others, partook of the nature of such a compromise as often takes place when public feeling, in regard to any established dogma, is only shaken without being absolutely changed.

Those who still held that a religion, the head of which they regarded as Antichrist, was a thing, the very existence of which constituted a national crime, were obliged to yield, in some degree, to the conviction of those who saw that an attempt to punish it as such, when professed by nearly a whole population, was an unavailing piece of atrocity, which would only render rebellion permanent, and endanger the security of the empire. The latter, on the other hand, while abolishing the penal laws, were constrained to leave unaltered other enactments which, while they fell short of absolute chastisement, still inflicted upon Roman Catholics, that host of less direct, but scarcely less galling, disabilities, involving the same principles of mistrust, hatred, and contempt on the part of the Government of the empire, and on that of their Protestant fellow-subjects.

If the abrogation of the penal code rendered possible the growth of a class of Irish Roman Catholics of superior wealth and education to that which hitherto existed, it had at the same time created an element of fresh and more dangerous hostility to the Government. The continued exclusion from that range of office to which men of talent, property and education aspire, necessarily produced a degree of irritation greater in proportion to their wealth and intelligence, and more formidable in proportion to the increased influence resulting from such acquisitions; while it furnished the lower classes, still disaffected and suffering from other grievances which more peculiarly affected their own condition, with leaders, influential, intelligent, and well furnished with all the arms of political warfare, many of them men of brilliant abilities, and smarting under the sting of unsatisfied ambition.

But the effects of these disabilities upon the

lower orders themselves, were in reality numerous and important; for although an exclusion from the higher offices of the State or of seats in Parliament, to which they could scarcely, under any circumstances pretend, did not immediately affect their condition, the stigma fixed upon the higher classes of their own religion, to whom they naturally looked up, wounded their pride, and confirmed them in the idea that they were still looked upon as a degraded caste.

The fact that the law, however just it might be in itself, was, when applied to them, administered solely by those who regarded them in that light, while their fellow-religionists, in whose sympathies they might confide, were rigorously excluded from office, begat or nourished in them a mistrust and hatred of all law, so profound and indiscriminate that it has been remarked, that a disposition to defy and evade its authority, irrespective of its bearing upon political or religious questions, had been engrafted on the national character to such an extent as to pervade all classes.

It would have been impossible to convince a Roman Catholic of the lower orders, that any case in which he and a Protestant were at issue, could by possibility be fairly decided by a Protestant judge or jury—that any question between him and a Protestant fellow-tenant would be impartially treated by a Protestant landlord. The knowledge that the law designedly excluded from the Bench the man who might befriend him, and excluded from the legislature the man who might represent his interests or sympathise with his feelings, was enough to fix for ever in his mind the deep-rooted conviction that from *that* law he could expect no justice, and that, consequently, to *that* law he owed no obedience. The reasoning of Romeo to the hesitating apothecary was applicable to his case—

> " Famine is in thy cheeks,
> Need and oppression starveth in thy eyes;
> Upon thy back hangs ragged misery;
> The world is not thy friend, nor the world's law;
> The world affords no law to make thee rich—
> Then be not poor, but *break it*, and take this."

In whatever language expressed, that such was the feeling of the great majority of the Irish people there can be no doubt.

" I do not think," said one of the witnesses at the Committee of 1825, " I ever spoke to a Catholic, high or low, that did not betray something like irritation on this subject." And the state of the country was thus described by Sir Robert Peel in his speech introducing the Emancipation Bill into the House of Commons :—

" A dreadful commotion distracts the public mind of Ireland ; a feverish agitation and unnatural excitement prevail to a degree scarcely credible throughout the whole country. Social intercourse is poisoned there in its very springs.

Family is divided against family, and man against his neighbour—in a word, the bonds of social life are almost dissevered, and the fountains of public justice corrupted. The spirit of discord walks openly abroad, and an array of physical force is marshalled in defiance of all law, and to the imminent danger of the public peace."*

Such, then, were the prevailing traditional and habitual sentiments of the Roman Catholics of Ireland, in reference to their connection with Great Britain, and their relations to their Protestant fellow-countrymen; and it was these, and the manifest evils which flowed from them, that the Catholic Emancipation Act was meant to mitigate, if not to cure.

That Act passed in the year 1829, and by it the oaths required to be taken by members of Parliament, and by the great majority of the officers of the State and the Judiciary, were modified in such a manner as to render them unobjectionable to a member of the Roman Catholic religion; the only Irish offices exempted being those of the Lord Lieutenant and Lord Chancellor.

Thus the access to those Parliamentary and official careers, from which they had been excluded by oaths which had been designedly inserted as tests, rendering it impossible for a Roman

---

* See Hansard's Parliamentary Debates, 1829, vol. xx.

Catholic to subscribe to them, was at once thrown open to persons of that persuasion.

We have, accordingly, seen members of the Roman Catholic Church in considerable numbers freely elected to serve in Parliament, and filling the highest offices in the Irish Judiciary; the clause by which the Chancellorship was excluded from the operation of the Act has since been repealed, and that high office is now filled by a Roman Catholic lawyer.

Much was hoped from the Act. It was sincerely the opinion of its warmest and most intelligent advocates that it was the great panacea by which all the ills of this ill-fated country would be cured—the one thing needful to its happiness and prosperity, the extirpation of the very root of its misfortunes and its crimes. In the heat of debate, and in the vehemence of the struggle, the anticipations of those most interested were almost boundless—in the words of one of its most talented and eloquent supporters, himself a Roman Catholic, and a sufferer in his professional career from the existing disabilities, it was expected that—

" Catholic emancipation would, by the removal of the causes for dissension, annihilate dissension itself; that it would banish those disastrous divisions which were the sources of not only national rancour, but of crime which, from its universality, became almost equally national ; that tranquillity would be speedily restored, and that peace would lead commerce and capital into a country from which an agitation, bordering upon insurrection, had made them exiles; that the distinctions between Protestants and Roman Catholics would almost instantaneously vanish, and the feeling of common citizenship would supersede the artificial and odious relations of sect in which men were placed to each other."*

Other declarations, not less decisive and not less eloquent, proceeded also from sources equally authentic, and claimed belief as coming from persons whose closest interests were involved. Nor is their sincerity to be questioned, although their expectations have not been realized in their full extent.

It would, indeed, be too much to say, that Catholic emancipation is a measure which has failed in its promised effect, and one which it would have been better never to have passed; but that its apparent results have fallen far short of the brilliant anticipations and disappointed the hopes, both of those who were the objects of the boon conceded, and of those who conceded it, there can be no doubt.

In the consideration, however, of the effects of any political measure, account must be taken of the evils which it has prevented, as well as of the

* See Essay on the "Effects of Emancipation," by R. L. Sheil.

good which it has effected. It is rarely, however, that the former are appreciated, or even noticed, by the general public. It requires more philosophy than is generally brought to bear upon such matters, to weigh quantities which have no visible existence, and the real existence of which may even be questioned.

In this case, however, we have the opinion of statesmen of the greatest sagacity then living, that the measure of Catholic emancipation was necessary to prevent, and did prevent, civil war. If we are constrained to the conclusion that more was necessary, that the whole case had not been met or grappled with, that innumerable sources of evil had been left untouched—we cannot, on the other hand, but recognize that Catholic emancipation was the necessary prelude to every other measure for the regeneration of Ireland, and that without which every attempt at real improvement must inevitably fail. The road, no doubt, has turned out to be a longer one than was expected; but it appears indubitable, that although the journey is far from being accomplished, the first stage of it, and that a long one, has been successfully travelled over, by the enactment of this all-important measure.

> " So pleased at first the towering Alps we try,
> Mount o'er the vales, and seem to tread the sky,
> Th' eternal snows appear already past,
> And the first clouds and mountains seem the last.

> But those attained, we tremble to survey
> The growing labours of the lengthen'd way,
> Th' increasing prospect tires our wandering eyes,
> Hills peep o'er hills, and Alps on Alps arise."

A period of comparative tranquillity followed the triumphant passage of the Act. It must be recollected that it was carried against a powerful opposition; that it had long been resisted by the highest governing powers of the State; the Sovereign himself was known to be indisposed to it at the best; the very statesmen comprising the administration which brought it forward were known to have been its determined and persistent opponents, and it now appeared only to have been wrested from them by the force of circumstances. Its fate, even in the last debates, hung long and dubiously in the balance. Its passage was a victory over an adversary who had been long considered to be invincible, and the brilliancy of the achievement tended, no doubt, to enhance the opinion which was held of the inherent benefits it was expected to confer, while the disappointment was proportionally greater, when they were found to be neither so great as was supposed, nor the rights acquired immediately available to their new possessors.

It was soon perceived that the whole social condition of a people, formed by wants and circumstances which had been in operation for ages, could not be at once reversed, or even essentially modified by one Act of Parliament, however comprehensive or important. It was felt, to use the words of an English statesman, Lord Brougham, that "the mere conferring of equal rights upon every class and sect would not suffice to satisfy the reasonable desires of the most moderate partizans of the excluded caste. To be eligible only, and never be elected; to be qualified by law, but excluded in practice; to be rendered capable of promotion, but never to be made partakers in the honours and emoluments attached to the public service, so far from an improvement in the condition of the Catholics, appeared rather a worse lot than that from which the Emancipation pretended to redeem them."

The sagacity of another English statesman was not at fault as to the probable effects of the measure:—

"Its promoters," observed Mr. Sadleir, in 1829, "had calmed the agitated surface of society, but had not heeded that fathomless depth of misery, sorrow, and distress, whose troubled waves still heaved unseen and disregarded."

Still, after the lapse of years, the spirit of emancipation has been diffused. In proportion as the state of society which prevented the extension of the benefits which it was intended to confer upon Catholics, became modified by the increase in wealth, in education, and in influence of persons of that persuasion, the rights which the law allowed were practically extended to them; and it cannot now with justice be said that any member of that communion, possessing the other requisites and qualifications for advancement in the offices of the State, or of the higher professions, is either excluded from or retarded in his career on account of his religion.

It is one of the natural laws of social life, which no legislation, without a forcible interference with the liberty of its subjects, could reverse, that high office, professional success, and the exalted and coveted positions of the world will, *cæteris paribus*, fall to the lot of the wealthy, the well-educated, the well-connected, or advantageously situated. This is a tendency which no enactment could, or ever has, altered for a continuance in any state. All the law can do in such cases is to allow the field to remain open to those who, by superior talents or good fortune, may attain such condition, and to refrain from placing artificial obstructions in the way of those who struggle for the prizes of life.

In Ireland, it was true, that the events of its past history, violent and unlucky as they were, had unjustly appropriated nearly all these advantages to one sect, while the other was excluded from the possibility of raising itself to their level. It was right that this distinction should be abolished; but it was unreasonable to suppose that the state of things which it had created would at once change. On the enactment of a law to that effect, the position of the two classes could not be suddenly equalized, still less could it suddenly be reversed. Yet it was the inevitable disappointment of these unfounded hopes which caused what is so generally, though, we think, erroneously, considered the failure of the measure of Catholic Emancipation.

CHAPTER VIII.

THE FORTY-SHILLING FREEHOLDERS.

THE enfranchisement of forty-shilling freeholders in 1793, and their subsequent disfranchisement, in connection with Roman Catholic emancipation, in 1829, are measures which have had so much influence on the condition of the peasantry of this country, that some attempt to trace their history and effects could scarcely be omitted in an investigation like the present.

One of the results of the civil and religious war which terminated by the establishment of the principles of the revolution of 1688, the principal and concluding scenes of which were, it must be borne in mind, enacted in Ireland, was the inevitable exclusion of Roman Catholics, and of Irish Roman Catholics more particularly, from all offices of the State, the Magistracy, and the Judiciary, as well as from seats in the English or Irish Parliament.

The *disfranchisement* of Roman Catholic electors seems to have taken place virtually, and as a matter of course, at the same time; for although it appears that they were not, until the year 1727, deprived by law of their right to vote for members of Parliament, it was ascertained by the Speaker of the Irish House of Commons, after a minute search, on the occasion of a debate in 1793, that they never had attempted to exercise it since the Revolution.* The existence of a doubt on the matter is, however, sufficient to establish the fact, that if the privilege had not been formally withdrawn by law, it had become practically a dead letter. However this may be, a total disfranchisement of the whole Roman Catholic body, no doubt, subsisted until the year 1788, when the policy of relaxing the penal disabilities affecting them was for the first time agitated.

The Catholic claims were taken up warmly, and with his usual vehemence and ability, by Mr. Burke, whose speeches and writings may be referred to for the arguments brought forward in their support; and his son, Richard Burke, acted under his direction with much zeal, as agent for the Irish Roman Catholics. Mr. Burke embodied and summed up his own views on the subject, by a memorable declaration on the occasion of Lord

---

* Life and Death of the Irish Parliament, by Chief Justice Whiteside.

Nugent's motion for a committee to consider the trade of Ireland, in the following words:—

"Ireland is *now** the chief dependence of the British Crown, and it particularly behoves this country to admit the Irish nation to the privileges of British citizens."

This important position does not then seem to have been met by a single dissentient voice in the Parliament of Great Britain.

The practical, or, at all events, the complete application of the principle was, nevertheless, destined to meet with an opposition deep-seated and persistent; and its illustrious advocate had long passed from the scene before the accomplishment of his design was effected.

Circumstances, which at first sight would have appeared likely to favour it, in reality served to retard it. The well-known Volunteer movement, which took place in the same year (1788), and in which Protestants and Roman Catholics seemed for a moment to have forgotten their dissensions in a burst of patriotic enthusiasm, aiming at no less an object than the entire independence of Ireland and of her Parliament from all control of the Parliament of Great Britain, appears, nevertheless, not to have extinguished, if it did not, indeed, rather revive, the religious differences

---

* "*Now*," in evident allusion to the loss of the North American Colonies, as he no doubt conceived, and perhaps truly, in consequence of the obstinate rejection of his conciliatory advice.

which disunited those who had participated in it, and continued to subsist among them, in regard to the admission of Roman Catholics to seats in the Legislature. An obstacle, too, of another nature, which was treated with great delicacy and reserve, but which was at that time considered to be very essential, was known to exist. A scruple was entertained, and, no doubt, conscientiously felt, by the reigning Sovereign, (George III.), as to whether the admission of Roman Catholic members to Parliament and other high offices of State could be reconciled with the terms of the oath he had taken at his coronation. Such a conviction in the mind of a man of his character was not likely to be easily shaken or neglected, and seemed to constitute an impassable barrier to the passage of any full measure of Catholic Emancipation during his reign.

The stupendous events, however, which were occurring in Europe, and more particularly the aggressive spirit and ambitious projects of revolutionary France, manifested by the dangerous "Propagandism" set on foot of the subversive doctrines then in vogue in that country—not unconnected, as the British Government must even then have been aware, with the spirit of rebellion which had been roused in Ireland — could not but press strongly upon the attention of the English Administration, the necessity of some measure founded upon the principle enounced by Burke, for the consolidation of the empire, by the conciliation of those classes of its subjects from which danger might be apprehended at such a crisis.

An Emancipation Bill was accordingly brought forward by the Government in the early part of the year 1793, and was passed.*

By this measure, penal disabilities were removed, and many concessions made to the Roman Catholics, of which the most important appeared to be the privilege conferred upon forty-shilling freeholders, irrespective of their religion, to vote for members of Parliament. The right of sitting in Parliament as members was, however, not conceded to persons of the Roman Catholic persuasion, and they were still debarred from holding the great offices of State, and from exercising many of the most important functions of the civil Government.

---

* "The Parliament met on the 10th January, 1793, when the Lord Lieutenant, (Lord Westmoreland,) after lamenting the spirit of discontent that had manifested itself in different parts of the kingdom, and having stated the ambitious and aggressive views of France, assured the Parliament that he had it in particular from his Majesty to recommend it to them to apply themselves to the consideration of such measures as might be most likely to strengthen and cement a general union of sentiment among all classes and descriptions of his Majesty's subjects, in support of the established constitution. With this view, his Majesty trusted that the situation of his Majesty's Catholic subjects would engage their serious attention, and in the consideration of this subject, he relied on the wisdom and liberality of Parliament."—(See Plowden's History of Ireland.)

The measure was, indeed, in this respect, an anomalous, and, as it proved, an unwise one. It has not escaped the discernment of the able author* of the " Life and Death of the Irish Parliament," that this emancipation, to be beneficial, ought to have been " begun at the opposite end of the social scale"—nor could it elude his penetration, that the alacrity of the Irish Parliament in adopting it proceeded from the short-sighted view of the landlords, that the ignorant mass of voters thus created would furnish them with tools for political ambition, rather than constitute a tribunal before which they would be responsible for their acts. Some of the bad consequences which did, and others which might have followed, this ill-conceived measure, were clearly pointed out by members of the Irish Parliament at the time; but it brought other social evils in its train which were not so easily foreseen, and to which we shall presently have to advert.

To the class, however, on which the franchise was conceded as a *boon*, it turned out to be anything but a *blessing*. Upon the more wealthy, intelligent, and enlightened portion of the Roman Catholic community, whose loyal co-operation in securing the safety of the country, it ought to have been the first object of an Emancipation Bill to secure, it conferred no benefit whatever—if it

---

* Chief Justice Whiteside.

did not, indeed, render their exceptional condition more galling and invidious than before.

Subsequent events have demonstrated that, as a measure for disarming an impending tempest, the Emancipation Bill of 1793, was lamentably inefficacious. The apprehended explosion took place in 1798, and proved to what an extent the ground had been previously undermined. In connection with it, Ireland was exposed, as had also been foreseen, to a foreign invasion; and if neither of these formidable blows aimed at the integrity of the empire were successful, much is to be attributed to Providential circumstances, such as had on former occasions helped to save England from similar attacks, and but little to the legislative Acts of either the British or Irish Parliament, or to the wise precautions of the Imperial Government. To the Protestants of Ireland, it must be admitted, was mainly owing, on that occasion, the preservation of the connection of their country with Great Britain.

The consequences of such events were obvious and unavoidable—the maintenance and reinforcement of the system known by the name of "Protestant Ascendancy," and the abandonment or indefinite postponement of all contemplated measures for the conciliation of the Roman Catholic part of the population of Ireland.

Such a result may be regretted, but it was inevitable. No other solution, which would not involve the disruption of the empire, was possible; and so much was this felt by the great statesman who ruled England at that momentous period, that it became clear to him that the re-establishment of Protestant ascendancy would be insufficient, and that if England and Ireland were to continue politically united, the *legislative union* of the two countries had become a necessary condition of their national co-existence.

When we reflect upon the nature and proportion of the great contest for empire in which England was so long engaged with France, and remember who was her antagonist, it may be a matter of surprise that even that measure secured from attack a point so weak as Ireland continued to be, and from which so deadly a blow might have been levelled at the power of Great Britain.

The accomplishment of this great object threw every other measure regarding the improvement of Ireland into the shade.

In the meantime, the effect of the enfranchisement of forty-shilling freeholders, which is, at present, more immediately the object of our attention, had conferred, as contemplated by the landowners, an almost indefinite power upon them, of creating voters at Parliamentary elections, who should be entirely under their control.

To so great a degree was this power abused, that masses of a peasantry, ignorant and degraded to the last degree, and possessing neither capacity or disposition for a safe or rational exercise of their new functions, or any motive other than the fear of incurring the displeasure of their landlord, were, to use a well-known phrase applied to them, driven like cattle by a salesman to the elections; or if any other influence was brought to bear upon them, it was that of the clergy of their own persuasion, who might, in order to secure the return of some member who, though a Protestant, (which was still a necessary condition till 1829,) might be supposed to be more liberally inclined, or less bigotedly opposed, to them than another. In such cases the unfortunate possessor of the forty-shilling franchise, fared ill between the temporal pains which he knew could be inflicted by his landlord, and the spiritual penalties which he believed might be the consequence of disobedience to his priest. The system of electioneering in Ireland, thus created, comprised nearly all the evils of universal suffrage in a country unfitted for such an institution, without any of its real or supposed advantages. It brought to the hustings crowds of voters utterly unqualified by their barbarous ignorance to form an opinion upon any political subject, while it failed to secure to them that kind of independence from corrupt influences which an indefinitely extended suffrage is calculated to bestow.

Practices objectionable in themselves, and productive of worse consequences, immediately arose from the abuse of the power thus conferred upon landed proprietors.

A passion for acquiring political influence developed itself among them, and was carried to excess by mutual rivalry. It even extended itself to other classes; and persons having no natural connection with the land, were known to speculate upon this kind of political capital. Not only were existing estates cut up into small holdings for the purpose of multiplying voters, but tracts of land—often unfit for cultivation—were enclosed and portioned out to fictitious forty-shilling freeholders. It was evident that low as that qualification was, it was not in reality the test which determined the power of voting, or limited the number of voters. In practice it could not be applied *bonâ fide;* and there was scarcely a holding too minute to be brought, by one contrivance or another, up to the supposed value of forty shillings, if the vote of its occupant was required. The power, in fact, of producing voters at an election was only limited by the means or activity of the landlord, and the numbers of grown-up men on an estate, whatever might be the degree of their poverty, ignorance or unfitness. The effects upon the people themselves were not less deplorable. Without dwelling upon the wholesale perjury and corruption attendant upon such a system, rioting, violence, intimidation, and excess presented themselves in their most revolting forms, and, together with drunkenness, quarrels, and idleness, so characterised the proceedings, not only of the lower orders, but too often of individuals of other classes, at elections, that an "Irish election" became almost the proverbial phrase by which everything that is demoralizing in assemblies of the kind was designated. Nor can it be said with truth, that the ultimate object of all methods of election, namely, the obtaining of a sufficient number of respectable representatives, qualified by independent position, talents, and acquirements to carry on the legislative business of a country, was more nearly attained by this system of apparently open voting, than by the sort of nomination described by Sir Lawrence Parsons, in the Irish Parliament, when the members knew nothing of the places they represented, or had ever seen their constituents.* Let the comparison not be thought invidious; but, we believe, that as regarded social position, capacity for business, or the more brilliant, though less essential, qualities of eloquence and wit, the old unreformed Parliament of Ireland was, to say the least, not inferior in those respects to that which has at any subsequent time been re-

* "A majority of this House never go back to their constituents; they do not know them; they do not live among them; many of them never saw them—no, nor even the places that they represent. What a mockery is this of representation! Do you think that in this enlightened age such an imposture can long continue? Impossible." (See Speech of Sir Lawrence Parsons, in the Irish Parliament, 1794, on the Reform Bill.—Irish Debates, vol. xiv.)

turned by the votes of the forty-shilling freeholders. The names of Grattan, Flood, Curran, Fitzgibbon, Sir L. Parsons, and numerous others, show that whatever are the well-founded objections to the system under which they were chosen, it had not the effect of excluding genius, ability, or patriotism from the councils of the nation.

Among the ill effects to be traced, in a great measure, to the enfranchisement of the forty-shilling freeholders, there is one to which we would particularly direct our readers' attention, because it has not been obliterated without the infliction of suffering, so severe and so long continued, that it can scarcely be said to have even yet totally ceased. We mean the minute division of the land into what may be denominated pauper-holdings—resorted to, as we have said, for the creation of votes, but productive, no doubt in concurrence with other causes to which we have adverted, of an amount of wretchedness and destitution almost unknown in any country during the present age—all the miseries, in short, attendant upon a population which has outrun its means of subsistence. Famine, epidemic disease, agrarian outrage, precipitate expatriation—things of which we have dim records in the meagre annals of the dark ages of the world, but which it was fondly hoped could not recur upon such a scale in our more civilized times, and under our more enlightened forms of government.

There can now be little doubt that the over-population of starving paupers, which it was the object of the Sub-letting Act to remove from the land—a disease which was only repressed by the bitter cures of famine, plague, and wholesale emigration—was in a great measure caused by the suicidal process of multiplying votes by the subdivision of holdings.

But the process was in more senses than one suicidal to those who initiated it. For not only did ruin, disorder, and misery, with its attendant crimes, take up their dwelling upon the lands of those who had recourse to it, but that very political influence which it had been hoped to secure by it was lost. The arms which they had forged with so much care fell into the hands of others who were their opponents, and threatened to be used against them with fatal effect. Their case resembled that of the wounded eagle, who saw that the arrow which had pierced him had been feathered from his own wing.

We have observed that the only influence, other than that of his landlord, to which the forty-shilling freeholders could be subject, was that of the clergy of his own persuasion. This appears, at first, to have been feeble, or to have been feebly exerted, but it had gradually and surely increased, and at length became formidable, if not predominant. To such an extent was this the case, that at the period when it was contemplated by the

Imperial Government to complete the measure of Catholic Emancipation begun in 1793, by the admission of Roman Catholics to sit in Parliament, it became evident that the entire political power of the Protestant proprietors of Ireland would be irretrievably swamped by the deluge of Catholic voters which they themselves had let loose, but which would now be under the exclusive influence of the Catholic clergy. If their emancipation had become inevitable, there was no salvation possible for the political principles of the Protestants, except by the means of the countervailing abrogation of the very measure which they had themselves devised for its preservation; and the disfranchisement of the forty-shilling freeholders, whom they had enfranchised in 1793, became the *sine quá non* to their reluctant admission of Catholic Emancipation in 1829. It was felt, indeed, in England, as well as in Ireland, even by those of the Liberal party who now advocated Catholic Emancipation, that an arrangement by which the elective franchise should at the same time be raised was a necessary complement to that great measure, nor could the Emancipation Bill have been carried through the Imperial Parliament, or have obtained the Royal Assent,* without it. A Bill

---

* George IV., on giving his not very willing assent to the Catholic Emancipation Act, is reported, by those probably who love good stories, to have said to the Duke of Wellington, "Well, Duke, I fear that the result of what we have now done will be, that you will go to hell, and I to Hanover."

was consequently passed simultaneously with that for Roman Catholic Emancipation, raising the qualification of voters to £10—a provision, it is superfluous to say, which was unsatisfactory to the Roman Catholic body in Ireland, but which was in reality in no way injurious to their true interests or those of the empire at large.

The admission of the necessity of this measure of disfranchisement as an indispensable supplement to the emancipation of the Roman Catholics, constitutes a remarkable, though tacit acknowledgment on the part of the British Government and Parliament of their real opinions in regard to the force of party animosity in Ireland, and of their entire want of confidence in the efficacy of Catholic emancipation to appease it; however confidently it had been urged both by those who sought it for themselves, and by those who were in favour of conceding it, that it would at once remove every trace of party distinction or jealousy, arising from difference of religion.

CHAPTER IX.

Tithes and Church Rates.

That peace, harmony, and submission to the law, which the promoters of Roman Catholic emancipation had promised, were not, as we have seen, realised.

The people, stirred up as they had been by a long-continued agitation, disappointed in their expectations as to the benefits they expected to reap from it, feeling only the hardships of their disfranchisement, which destroyed the last inducement for landlords to keep them on the land, were but little disposed to embrace habits of subordination and contentment, to which they had been hitherto strangers. The great social changes which were slowly yet surely effected, shook to its very base the whole fabric of society in Ireland, and the lower orders, plunged in the depths of distress and poverty, were ready to have recourse to any way of bettering their condition.

The agitation which had resulted in Roman Catholic emancipation was not permitted to die out, and the feeling of disappointment at its effects was turned with renewed vigour to a matter affecting the people more immediately, namely, the payment of tithes.

Tithe was the money collected by law for the payment of the Protestant clergy of Ireland. It consisted of one-tenth of the produce of the land, and theoretically was to be paid " in kind." As this, however, was inconvenient, the whole produce was valued, and one-tenth of its value was paid in money. It was leviable on nearly every description of produce, although in different parts of the country there were some slight differences as to the articles. This tax, therefore, by falling upon the cultivators of the soil, threw the whole weight of the maintenance of the Protestant clergy upon the lower classes, the great majority of whom were Roman Catholics. Their poverty rendered the pressure of any tax severe, and it is easily understood that this one was more peculiarly odious to them. Indeed, on all sides, there were objections to it. To the Roman Catholics, it was odious that any payment should be made directly by the Catholic peasant, for the support of the Protestant clergyman. But even by the Protestants, objections were made because of abuses respecting the plurality of livings, the absence of the clergy from their parishes, and the unnecessary number of bishops. Nor was this to be wondered at, the more especially as tithe not unfrequently went to swell the purse of an absentee ecclesiastic.*

The burthen, moreover, was conceived to be heavier than it really was, from the payment being required directly out of the fruits of the industry of the occupiers, independent of its being avowedly devoted to an object hostile to their faith. Nor was this tax usually taken into account by the lower classes when bidding for land. They thought then only of the *rent*, and when called upon for tithe were, of course, always unwilling, and in many cases unable to pay it.

There was, consequently, no species of tax so difficult to collect, and none which caused so much irritation in the minds of the people. In point of fact, as we have seen from the earliest period, confusion and bloodshed had attended its enforcement.

"The system," say the Committee of the House of Commons, in their Report on Tithes, in 1832, " under which tithes were collected, especially in a country so circumstanced as Ireland, was highly

* Lord Brandon—a rector, about the year 1825—held livings to the amount of £2,000 a year, and was an absentee, whilst to a curate who did the work, an allowance was made insufficient for his support.

unfavourable, not more to the progress of agricultural improvement, than to the interests of religion and morality, and to the cultivation of those friendly feelings between a clergyman and his parishioners, which are essential to render their intercourse mutually beneficial."

The method generally in use was as follows:—Two persons were appointed by the clergyman for the valuation of the crops, which was usually made in July, often when they looked best; and these two persons were then sworn before a magistrate as to their valuation.

The amount of the tithe was not, however, then made known to the person upon whom it was levied, and the occupiers were left in a state of uncertainty both as to the sum and as to the time of payment, until the collectors came round, which they did not do until they thought the crops were sold.

The evidence of a gentleman before the Committee from whose report an extract has been made above, although, perhaps, describing an extreme case, gives an illustration of what was constantly occurring:—*

"When tithe is charged by the barrel (that is, a measure of produce) there is every room for imposition. In the first place, two tithe valuators go into a field, and one of them says, 'I value it at

* Evidence of Mr. William Collis, Q. 5139, Tithe Committee, House of Commons, 1832.

eighty barrels;' the other says, 'I value it at sixty.' 'Then let us split the difference.' That is the only mode of valuation. There is no kind of attempt to calculate. Then the clergyman says, 'I will not tell you what I will charge till Christmas time'—that is, I will not charge the lowest, which is the price it bears at the time of harvest, but I will tell you at Christmas time what I will charge. This is the way in which it is done in the county of Wexford."

Like rent, tithes often got into arrear; and as they also were recoverable by distress, the same consequences ensued.

Nor had the tithe-payers any means of controlling an unreasonable demand on the part of the tithe-owner, except by giving the tenth in produce instead of in money, and thus causing him much inconvenience. The crops, moreover, could not be sold until the valuator came round; for if the farmer carried away any part of the produce before that time, he was completely at the mercy of the tithe-owner—whatever the valuator then swore was the value, the occupier had to pay.

Thus, not only was tithe objected to on principle, but every detail connected with levying it was carried out in so obnoxious a manner as to rouse the people into open and violent opposition.

Disputes, accordingly, were constantly occurring, and were attended with animosities, much of the odium and discredit of which fell upon the clergy.

Finding the greatest difficulty in obtaining their tithes, they were obliged to resort to the still more injurious system of employing proctors—persons of desperate characters and fortunes—whose exercise of the large powers entrusted to them materially aggravated the evils of the system itself.*

It was to tithes what sub-letting was to land, the proctors taking the place of the middlemen. Nor was the name of tithe-proctor less generally detested. They took leases of the tithes from the clergy, giving exactly one-tenth to those they farmed them from, calculating for the profit on whatever above the tenth they could extract from the occupier of the land. Thus a great stimulus was given to extortion, and the greatest cruelties were perpetrated.

"I," said a witness before the Select Committee of 1832, " have known potatoes to be sold out of the house of poor people, and I have known the pot to be sold. I have known blankets to be taken off the beds of the children. I have known the widow's pig taken away, and I have known an aged widow taken out of a sick-bed, and laid on the ground, and the clothes, and the bed, and the daughter's clothes, sold for tithes."

* House of Commons Committee on Tithes, 1832.

Severities such as these could not but reflect upon the character of the laws by which they were inflicted.

Tithe became at length the source of such frightful crimes, and of so much bitterness and ill-feeling, that in the year 1824 a law was passed which was intended to remove some of its evils.

This was the Tithe Composition Act (4 Geo. IV., cap. 99, and its amendments.) By it the Lord Lieutenant of Ireland was empowered, upon a certain application being made to him, to give orders for the assembly of a special vestry in the parish for carrying the Act into execution. A Commissioner was then elected by the owners and occupiers of land, to treat with one named by the incumbent. The Commissioners were then to cause a survey and valuation to be made of the land and tithes in the parish, and to agree to a *fixed* sum, which the incumbent was to receive annually as a composition for all tithes. Such composition to continue for twenty-one years. The owners of land in any parish for the tithes of which composition was made under this Act, were to let such land thereafter tithe free, and the occupier paying the composition was to deduct it out of his rent.

It thus laid down the principles that tithe should no longer be a tax on the industry and capital of the occupying tenant, but that it should be converted into a rent-charge; that the rent-charge should be a fixed payment, at least varying only with the price of corn; and that it was payable, not by the occupying tenant, but by the landlord—a proportionate reduction from the amount of tithe being made in favour of the landlord who took the benefit of the Act, in consideration of the new responsibility to which he was subjected.

The Act was, however, unfortunately only optional, parishes being left the choice of adopting its provisions.

In those parishes which did adopt them, many of the grievances of the tithe system were done away with. The exactions and extortions of the proctors were put an end to. The cause of complaint as to the uncertain and fluctuating nature of the tax was removed, and tithe ceased to be a tax upon capital and industry, and became a moderate assessment on land.

By this latter change a transfer, or rather an equalization of the burthen, between the grazier and the cottier was effected, for in most parts of the country grass lands paid no tithe.

This was in itself a great boon to the cottiers, while the custom which prevailed throughout Ireland, of breaking up the whole of the land periodically, rendered it less injurious to the former than it would have been in a country where lands are permanently laid down in grass.

The effect was, undoubtedly, to give a considerable stimulus to tillage, and to bring into cultivation much land which would not have borne the charge of tithe, but which, having been of little value at the time of the composition, was charged for twenty-one years with a very low assessment.*

Thus nearly all of the complaints would have been removed, had the Act been carried into immediate and general operation. But this was not done, and more than seven years after its enactment, only two-thirds of the parishes in Ireland had adopted its provisions.†

The abuses which had before prevailed continued, therefore, through a great part of the country, and contributed to make every one discontented with tithe, so much so, that even those who had effected composition became dissatisfied with their position. The point now taken advantage of by them was, that while the Act provided that, in all future leases, the receipt of the clergyman for the tithe paid by the occupier should be taken by the landlord in payment of so much rent, it left the amount of tithe specified and distinct, as a charge directly payable by the occupying tenant of one religion to the clergyman of another. The actual occupiers of the soil, there-

* Report of House of Commons' Committee on Tithes, 1832.
† There were 2,312 parishes in Ireland, in 1,505 of which the provisions of the Acts of 1823 and 1824 had taken effect. (See same Report.)

fore, still remained immediately liable to the payment, which, in many instances, was collected in minute sums from a great number of persons, and thus the same unfortunate contact between the occupier and the clergyman continued to exist, and the tenant was led to forget that, if discharged from the payment of tithe, he would be called upon for an additional rent from his landlord, and to consider that payment, not as a charge upon the land but as a burthen upon himself. There was also the real inconvenience—and with the Irish inconveniences are but too commonly grievances—accompanying this, of the two sums, of rent and tithe, being demanded at different times by different people; and independent of these repeated demands, the small occupier who might not have at his command even the trifling sum due to the clergyman, was in case of enforcement of payment, or of legal proceedings against him, subject to an expense altogether disproportioned to the sum he was called on to pay.*

---

* In the House of Commons' Committee it is stated:—
" In amount the burthen of tithe throughout Ireland, as compared with the value of land, is in reality extremely light."
Upon a very careful and laborious calculation, the average of tithe composition was computed to be as follows:—

Ulster,	0s. 11½d. per acre,	or to rental	$\frac{1}{19}$ to	$\frac{1}{25}$
Munster,	1s. 2½d. per Irish acre,	,,	$\frac{1}{15}$ to	$\frac{1}{21}$
Leinster,	1s. 7½d. ,,	,,	$\frac{1}{15}$ to	$\frac{1}{21}$
Connaught, 0s. 10½d.	,,	,,	$\frac{1}{20}$ to	$\frac{1}{31}$

"The general result," say the Committee of the House of Lords in their Report on Tithes, (1832) "is, that from the defective operation of the system, the tithe-payer conceives himself to be subject to a degree of pressure, far greater than the actual amount of the sum paid by him would create; while the clergy who are entitled to the tithe have reaped a profit considerably less than the sum payable by the occupier of the land, and attended with circumstances no less unsatisfactory and painful to their own feelings, than detrimental to the public peace and happiness."

In most parts of the country the opposition to the payment of tithe had become systematic, and was pressed forward with such vigour, that it became quite as strong in those places where the Composition Act was in force as where it was not. Other circumstances, too, were strengthening the objections to it.

The political movement in England was not without some effect in Ireland.

"During the discussion produced by the Reform Bill," says the Annual Register of 1831, "the Church of Ireland had been spoken of in terms, which rendered it impossible for a populace otherwise perfectly disposed to such ideas to regard her in any other light than that of an unrighteous and wicked oppressor."

Payment of this obnoxious impost was everywhere resisted, and the usual system of threats and murder were resorted to. The process-servers could only perform their duty under strong escorts. When attempts were made to seize the property of the debtor, the whole country was in arms; the cattle or other live stock disappeared; every hill had a scout, who gave warning of the approach of the distrainers; and when it happened that the cattle were seized, no one dared to purchase them, no matter at what price, so great was the hatred to the law, or the fear of incurring the hostility of the people. The civil authorities were often not strong enough to cope successfully with the disturbances, and whenever the officers of the law interfered, open and bloody war was declared against them. The clergyman dared not ask; the willing occupier dared not pay. The most frightful scenes were enacted; the most awful and revolting crimes were perpetrated. It is unnecessary to enumerate them. Their result was stated by the Archbishop of Dublin in his evidence before the House of Commons' Tithe Committee:—" As for the continuance of the tithe system, it must be at the point of the bayonet—it must be through a sort of chronic civil war."

In this strait it was hoped that by spreading the benefits of the Composition Act, the country would be somewhat quieted; and, in the year 1832, a bill was accordingly passed, (2 & 3 William IV., cap. 119,) making the adoption of the

Tithe Composition Act compulsory, and the composition permanent. But this came too late. The time when such an enactment would have been beneficial had gone by. Throughout the country large anti-tithe meetings were held, and the measure tended neither to mitigate the discord nor diminish the crimes which that discord produced.

As a consequence of this resistance, the clergy had, in many instances, been reduced to great distress. With a deep sense of the necessity of recovering their rights, but with the deep sense also of the responsibility of resorting to extremities, they had abstained from adopting the offer of the Government, to use the strongest measures for the enforcement of their claims, and had preferred to encounter the distress which followed. As no payment could be obtained from the people, it was necessary to make some provision for the clergy; and a Bill was passed in the year 1833, (3 & 4 Wm. IV., cap. 100, commonly called "The Million Act,") advancing one million sterling, in order to relieve those of them who were in the greatest distress. As a security for repayment, the power to levy the arrears was transferred from the clergy to the Crown. This answered for a time; but it became evident that, with a view to secure both the interests of the Church and the welfare of the country, a permanent change of system was required, and that such a change to be safe and satisfactory must involve a complete extinction of tithes. This was proposed to be done either, by commuting them for a charge upon the land, or by an exchange for or an investment in land, but in whichever way accomplished, the revenues of the Church (as far as related to tithe) were to be effectually secured, and at the same time all occasions of pecuniary collisions removed between the parochial clergy and the occupiers of the land.

A Bill was accordingly introduced in 1834, proposing the commutation of the composition of tithes into a rent-charge, payable by the owners of estates; and as the liability was removed to those who possessed the chief interest in the land, and it was considered but just to make some compensation for the additional trouble they incurred, a reduction was proposed to be made in the amount of tithe which was to be levied off the land-owner, whilst the tithe which was paid by the occupier ceased to be paid as tithe to the landlord, but was paid as an increase of rent in one bulk sum. Unfortunately, however, owing to the leading feature of the Bill being the appropriation to general Irish uses of the surplus to be obtained, by reducing the Church establishment, the Bill was defeated.

Disturbances in regard to tithe still continued; but the position of the clergy in this respect had, in the meantime, greatly improved; for, while the measure each year was brought forward in Parliament and rejected, a system of levying payment, by exchequer process had been resorted to. This process compelled the police, and even the military, to give full assistance to those levying tithe, making them responsible, under heavy penalties, for the execution of the duties they were directed to perform. The force employed accordingly was too powerful to be resisted, and this mode of obtaining payment proved successful. Four years passed away; and at last, in the year 1838, upon the final abandonment of the surplus and appropriation clauses, the Bill became law as a mere commutation measure. (1 & 2 Victoria, cap. 109.)

This Act embodied the intentions already stated. Composition for tithes was abolished, and in lieu thereof, an annual rent-charge, equal to three-fourths of the old composition, was laid on the land, and was to be paid by the owner instead of by the occupier. Tithe, thus merged into rent, wholly disappeared, and became a tax upon the land, instead of upon its produce.

Thus was the settlement of a long-vexed question effected, in a manner beneficial to all parties concerned.

To the clergy, it gave the security and facility of obtaining what was due to them.

The landlord profited by a reduction of twenty-five per cent., a profit which was shared in by the tenantry, and they were no longer subject to the vexations incident upon collection.

It simplified all future contracts between landlord and tenant, the latter having henceforth to consider simply the rate of rent when about to enter into a lease.

The immediate effects of the measure, too, were highly gratifying. The irritation which had so long existed at once subsided. One source of agitation was completely extinguished; and from the time of the passing of the Act, there ceased to be any need for the employment of the services of the military or of the police in regard to tithe.

There was another tax to which we must refer here—one somewhat similar to tithe, and which excited even greater discontent, although upon a smaller scale. This was the parochial taxation for Church rates, which was levied upon the occupant of the land.

The Committee of the House of Commons, in their report upon tithes, observe:—

"The levy of Church cess for the building and repair of churches, and for the due celebration of Divine worship, is a tax trifling in amount, but peculiarly difficult of collection—peculiarly obnoxious to the feelings, not only of the Roman Catholic, but of a great proportion of the Protestants of Ireland, and of which the advantages to the Established Church are far more than counterbalanced by the odium attending its enforcement."

These rates, however, did not so long remain unaltered as tithes, having been abolished in 1833 by the Church Temporalities Act, (3 and 4 Wm. IV., cap. 37;) but this being a measure which, for the most part, regarded the internal constitution of the Church, it is unnecessary here to enter into a consideration of its other provsions.

CHAPTER X.

NATIONAL EDUCATION.

THE serious attention of the Government had, for many years, been turned to the education of the Irish people, and the necessity of improving it had long been recognised.

At an early period, the amount of crime in Ireland had been considered by the Legislature to be in a great degree proportionate to the ignorance of the people, and education was relied upon as productive of moral improvement, and thereby tending to aid the purposes of civil government.

Much of the poverty, also, of the country was attributed to the same cause; and it was hoped that a better education would produce the appreciation and the desire of an improved condition.

The means and appliances available for the education of the poor in Ireland had hitherto been very imperfect. In the northern and eastern parts of the country, the same superiority in regard to agriculture, and trade, and the general condition of the people, was observed to exist in regard to education. Schools were more numerous and efficient. The ideas of the people seemed, in consequence, to have become more enlarged, and their conduct better regulated. But in the southern and western parts, where the country was behindhand in those respects, education was but little advanced. In a great many places, English was a strange language, Irish being still spoken exclusively in extensive districts. A desire, however, on the part of the people to obtain education for their children seemed to be great and universal, and the children themselves may be said to have participated in it—a fact testified both by the number who frequented the schools, such as they were, and by the number of those schools; but the amount of knowledge imparted by them was small, and their organization was defective.

The great body of the children of the poor were, in fact, educated in what were called hedge or pay schools, and but few comparatively in schools supported in part or in whole by grants of public money, or by private subscriptions. In the year 1826, it was stated that the number of scholars in all the schools then existing was over 550,000. But, in conjunction with this apparently considerable diffusion of instruction, there existed the grossest popular ignorance. The education given was, in truth, more apparent than real. In the hedge schools more particularly, very little was taught; and in regard to moral and intellectual training, they were on the lowest possible scale. They had neither competent teachers nor proper books. In general, the schoolmasters themselves were unable to teach even reading and writing correctly; and such of them as could do so, were incapable of applying this elementary instruction in such a manner as could produce general information or moral improvement. Their smattering of knowledge sufficed, unfortunately, in many instances, to qualify them to figure as petty political agitators, local demagogues, or mischievous disturbers of the public peace.

Among the other schools, those most instrumental in diffusing knowledge were established by the well-known Kildare-place Society.*

This society had been founded in the year 1811, for the purpose of promoting the education of the poor in Ireland, by assisting in the foundation and support of schools, upon the principle that the appointment of teachers and the admission of scholars should be uninfluenced by religious distinctions, but in which, however, it was a condition, *sine quá non*, that the Bible, without note or comment, should be read. This system was consi-

* It was the first Society that ever attempted to establish in Ireland a higher class of schoolmasters, and to supply a better description of books.

dered by its founders to be impartial, and free from any suspicion of proselytism; but this opinion was not concurred in by the Roman Catholic clergy. It met, however, with the approval of the Government, so much so, that public grants were accorded to it annually, in aid of the private contributions to its support. These schools indubitably proved of considerable use; the education given in them was sound, and they were frequented by a large number of children.

There existed also parish and charter schools, and schools kept up exclusively for Roman Catholics by private subscription.

Still, although there might appear to be sufficient means of instruction, it was evident to all who were practically acquainted with the subject, that the object of an impartial, sound, and generally diffused education of the lower classes in Ireland was not attained; in the first place, because of the defective organization of the greater part of the schools, and in the second, from the sectarian or denominational character by which all of them were marked.

The object of the Government was how to devise a scheme of education depending on State support, and consequently under State control, yet, at the same time, on the general principle that the benefits of the system should be open to every class and denomination of his Majesty's subjects, without religious distinction, and above all, without any condition which would, in the opinion of any sect, imply a purpose, or afford an opportunity of influencing or interfering with the convictions of the different religionists who might frequent the schools.

That such were the views entertained by the Legislature, appears from the following extracts from the reports of the Committees of the House of Commons appointed for the investigation and consideration of this subject.

" No plan of education," say the Committee of 1812, " however wisely and unexceptionally contrived in other respects, could be carried into effectual operation in Ireland, unless it was especially avowed and clearly understood that no attempt should be made to influence or disturb the peculiar religious tenets of any sect or denomination of Christians."

And the Committee of 1824 observe:—

" In a country where mutual divisions exist between different classes of the people, schools should be established for the purpose of giving to children of all religious persuasions such useful instruction as they might severally be capable and desirous of receiving, without having any ground to apprehend any interference with their respective religious principles."

They continue also:—

" It is expedient to devise a system of mutual education, from which suspicion should, if possible, be banished, and the causes of distrust and jealousy should be effectually removed; and under which the children might imbibe similar ideas, and form congenial habits, tending to diminish, not to increase, that distinctness of feeling now but too prevalent."

A few years afterwards, another Committee was appointed to take these previous reports into their consideration, and having done so, they observe:—

"It is of the utmost importance to bring together children of the different religious persuasions in Ireland, for the purpose of instructing them in the general subjects of moral and literary knowledge, and providing facilities for their *religious* instruction *separately*, when differences of creed render it impracticable for them to receive religious instruction together.

"This plan cannot be objected to as disconnecting religion from morality and learning; on the contrary, it binds them together indissolubly, and appears to unite them in a manner suited to the principles of sound policy, good faith, and Christian charity."

It was upon the principles, therefore, laid down in these reports, and generally accepted by public opinion in England, that the plan for the establishment of National Education in Ireland was framed; and after ample discussion, finally sanctioned in 1832, by a grant of money for the support of the proposed system, which sum was to be intrusted to the Lord Lieutenant, to be expended under the superintendence of Commissioners appointed by the Crown. In the meantime, the Government had addressed to the Duke of Leinster in 1831, a letter, stating their intention to constitute a Board for the superintendence of National Education in Ireland, and proposing to place his Grace at its head. The powers of the Board, the objects which it was intended to effect, the manner in which the money to be voted by Parliament was to be expended, the arrangements relative to the formation of schools, and other particulars, were explained in this letter.

Thus was established in Ireland a system of education which, although it has undergone several modifications, still remains in force in regard to all its main features.

It has consequently been now under trial for more than thirty-five years; and it will be for us to examine how far it may have answered the expectations of those who devised it; how far its immediate objects have been achieved or have failed in success; and more especially, in how far the great end proposed by every system of public education, of facilitating the purposes of civil government by an improvement in morals, has been arrived at.

It is evident that, in the application of a system of National Education to Ireland, two objects were held in view, both highly desirable in themselves, both conceived in a liberal and conciliatory spirit, but, when combined, of extreme difficulty in their attainment.

The one was to afford the means of access to a sound and efficient moral, intellectual, and technical instruction to all classes of the people of Ireland. The other, to unite, upon the common ground of such instruction, the rising generation of a people so long divided by a difference of religious creed, and by political antipathies consequent upon the events of its stormy by-gone history. It was hoped, and not unnaturally, that in an association for the pursuit of knowledge, prejudices would be worn down, animosities die out, and that in an exchange of good offices, it would at length be found that divergence of religion did not necessarily involve hatred and distrust, or contempt of all those who professed opposing dogmas; that religious convictions might safely be left to the conscience of each individual, and to the spiritual pastors of each sect; while all might combine in the cultivation of those faculties which are so well known to soften the asperities of life.

> "Ingenuos didicisse fideliter artes,
> Emollit mores nec sinit esse feros"—

is a trite, but not less pregnant remark; nor was it unreasonable to entertain the hope, that the truth of the maxim would be exemplified in a country where the natural capacity for intellectual improvement is great, and has never failed to develop itself with unusual brilliancy, whenever circumstances have enabled any individual to relieve himself from the pressure of the comparative ignorance, poverty, and barbarity, which has for ages weighed upon his country.

As regards the first of the two objects of which we have spoken, namely, the establishment of a greater number of efficient schools, and the numbers educated in them, the reports of the Commissioners and the documents laid before Parliament afford us valuable information.

Immediately upon the appointment of the Commissioners, the Board was opened for applications for assistance. They came in considerable numbers, and grants were made accordingly. Many of the schools which had formerly been hedge schools were absorbed by those of the National Board. The schools gradually increased, and the number of pupils each year grew larger. The second report of the newly-appointed Commissioners shows that the progress which had been made in the new system was in their opinion highly satisfactory. The third report states that considerable advance had been made in the buildings, and marks a further increase in the number of schools and pupils.

Progress at first, however, appears to have been slow. Great difficulties had to be surmounted; the inability or carelessness of many of the local patrons, the ignorance of the teachers, the poverty of the people, and the opposition of many persons of position and influence, were hindrances which were not easily surmounted.

By far the greater number of the schools connected with the National Board had formerly been hedge schools, and at the commencement of the National system great difficulty was found in obtaining teachers. For some years, consequently, the masters in the National Schools were not above those of the hedge schools, nor the schools themselves much better. By degrees, however, a better class of masters was obtained; and after some years, a training school for masters and mistresses was formed, and a marked improvement in this respect took place.

A great difference was noticeable in the results attained in proportion to the rate of expenditure.

In 1825, under the old plan, the State granted £68,718 for education, and the number of children educated was 69,638. Under the Commissioners of National Education, in 1837, the grant for the year was £50,000, and the number of children on the lists of the schools, 169,000.

The following return gives the number of schools and pupils on the rolls, under the superintendence of the Commissioners, since the commencement of the system, and the amount of Parliamentary grants annually voted for its maintenance :—

Years.	No. of Schools.	No. of Pupils.	Parlmtary Grants.	Years.	No. of Schools.	No. of Pupils.	Parlmtary. Grants.
1833	789	107,042	£25,000	1852	4,875	544,604	£182,073
1834	1,106	145,521	35,000	1853	5,023	550,631	193,040
1835	1,181	153,707	35,000	1854	5,178	551,110	215,200
1836	1,300	166,929	35,000	1855	5,124	535,905	227,641
1837	1,384	169,548	50,000	1856	5,245	560,134	213,030
1838-9	1,581	192,971	100,000	1857	5,337	776,473	257,641
1840	1,978	232,560	50,000	1858	5,408	803,610	273,030
1841	2,337	281,849	57,000	1859	5,496	806,510	270,722
1842	2,721	319,792	55,000	1860	5,632	804,000	285,377
1843	2,912	355,320	55,000	1861	5,830	803,364	290,904
1844	3,153	395,550	75,000	1862	6,010	812,527	269,377
1845	3,426	432,844	85,000	1863	6,163	840,569	346,904
1846	3,637	456,410	100,000	1864	6,263	870,401	316,770
1847	3,825	402,632	120,000	1865	6,372	922,084	325,582
1848	4,109	507,469	125,000	1866	6,453	910,819	336,130
1849	4,321	480,623	120,000	1867	6,520	913,198	344,700
1850	4,547	511,239	140,000	1868	6,586	967,563	360,195
1851	4,704	520,401	164,577				

The average daily attendance for the year 1867 was 321,683; for the year 1868, 354,853.

On the whole, therefore, after some years' experience, it was not unfairly concluded, that a considerable degree of success had attended the system of National Education in regard to one of its objects; and that a very much greater amount of instruction of a better quality had been diffused among a greater number of the population than by any of the previously existing schools, and at a reduced rate of comparative cost.

It was, consequently, the opinion of successive administrations that no effort should be spared to encourage and, if possible, enforce its general adoption.

With respect to the other object to which we have alluded as being contemplated by the system, it cannot now be concealed that its results have not been by any means so satisfactory.

In places where the Roman Catholics predominated, the great majority of the children sent to the schools were naturally of that persuasion; in which cases the children of such Protestants as might have resorted to them were rapidly withdrawn; and the instruction given in them either became, or was believed to have become, so entirely sectarian in character as to render it inconsistent with, or hostile to, the doctrines of the reformed religion.

In some instances, indeed, the schools under these circumstances were known to be in open connection with the ministers of the Roman Catholic Church, and even in certain cases the children were taught by nuns, clad in the dress of their order. (House of Lords' Committee on Education, 1837.) In Ulster, on the other hand, and in parts of the country where there was a sufficiently large Protestant population, the schools were frequented numerously by the children of that persuasion; but when this occurred, the attendance of Roman Catholic children was, and still is, denounced and forbidden by the clergy of that Church, as dangerous and infectious to the purity of their faith; and in no instance was the presence of Roman Catholic children in the National Schools authorized by their clergy, except where the pupils of that persuasion composed them "in toto," or were in an overwhelming majority, and the management and teaching were practically under the exclusive control of Roman Catholic teachers, and the supervision of Roman Catholic priests.*

* The following table exhibits the number of children of each religious persuasion attending the schools in the year 1868:—
 70,302 or 7.27 were of the Established Church,
 782,984 or 80.93 were Roman Catholics,
 107,401 or 11.10 were Presbyterians,
  6,757 or 0.70 were of other persuasions.

From the returns which had been received on the publication of the thirty-fifth report by the Commissioners of National Education, it appears that there were:—3,837 mixed schools, or those in which the pupils were of different persuasions; and 2,626 unmixed schools, of which 206 were exclusively Protestant, (24,182 pupils,) and 2,420 were exclusively Roman Catholic (having 384,672 pupils.)

The following summary shows the extent to which mixed education prevails in Ireland, and the proportions of pupils of the respective religions attending the schools:—

119,817 Protestants mixing with 30,895 Roman Catholic pupils, in 1,122 schools, taught exclusively by Protestant teachers; giving to each school an average of 106.8 Protestants to 27.6 Roman Catholics.

14,415 Protestants with 12,327 Roman Catholics, in 120 schools, taught conjointly by Protestant and Roman Catholic teachers; giving to each school an average of 120.1 Protestant and 102.7 Roman Catholic pupils.

26,046 Protestants with 354,764 Roman Catholics, in 2,595 schools, taught exclusively by Roman Catholic teachers; giving to each school an average of 10.0 Protestant to 136.7 Roman Catholic pupils.

Protestants predominate in 1,129 schools, and have 206 schools exclusively to themselves. Roman Catholics predominate in 2,708 schools, and have 2,420 exclusively to themselves. (See thirty-fifth report of the Commissioners of National Education, for 1868.)

It thus became evident that the conciliatory intention of the Imperial Government had in this respect been completely frustrated. The schools, instead of being, as was intended, *general*, had become in reality *denominational;* and instead of affording a common ground for the formation of congenial habits, and the removal of mutual distrust, had but too often served to mark out distinction and embitter jealousy, without, it is almost needless to remark, satisfying the aspirations, or conciliating the good-will of either of the religious and political parties which it was meant to unite.

It was in vain that the statesmen of England and the great functionaries of the British Government—who, from want of a just appreciation of the real state of religious feeling in Ireland, were unable to comprehend why a measure apparently so fair and so conciliatory should be obstructed—exerted every effort, and used every influence in its behalf. Motives of interest were found insufficient to gain over a sufficient number of the clergy of the Established Church, to act as a body in its support, while the pretensions of the Roman Catholic clergy were not to be satisfied, or their suspicions lulled, by any middle term which could be devised. If the grants of the Board of Education were a gift in which they were allowed to partake, and in many instances almost to monopolize, they were, nevertheless, regarded as the gift of an opponent.

"Timeo Danæos et dona ferentes" expresses a feeling, which, unfortunately, still too much prevails among the members of that body, in regard even to the most liberal boons and concessions from Protestant England.

It is to be observed, that one of the most steadfast advocates of the National School system, the learned and liberal Protestant Archbishop of Dublin, Doctor Whately,* whose efforts had been unceasing, and, as he for a long time flattered himself, successful, in eliminating, in concurrence with the Roman Catholic Archbishop who sat with him on the Commission, every element of difference, was compelled at length to throw up the game, and to withdraw his important support and countenance from the National Schools, from which he, with others, had hoped to derive such happy results.

On the other hand, one of the leading prelates of the Roman Catholic Church in Ireland, and one

---

* In his examination before the Committee of the House of Lords, which sat in 1854, to inquire into the progress made by the National School system, the Archbishop of Dublin said:— "I approve of the principle of the system most completely. The system has succeeded in every instance where it has had a fair trial; but there was a very strong prejudice against it, arising from a great variety and combination of circumstances. A system which has been flourishing with unexpected success for more than twenty years."

O

whose declaration would be likely to have the greatest possible weight with all of his persuasion, has gone so far as to announce that he rejected the system " in toto," as being dangerous to the faith and morals of his flock.*

In order to account for the failure of this part of the well-intended plan of Government, it must be borne in mind, that both Protestants and Roman Catholics in Ireland agree, nay insist, that any system of moral training to be effective or acceptable to them must necessarily be founded upon *religion;* and in this opinion they are supported by the nearly unanimous voice of the English public and of the Imperial Legislature. It is needless to say, that he who enounces this doctrine means by " religion" that form of the Christian religion which he himself deems to be the true one; and that if he considers it to be essential that moral education should be founded

---

* At a speech made in Wexford by Cardinal Cullen, he is reported to have said :— . . . . " The question of education is so important, that on it depends the future fate of religion in our country. . . . I have not ceased to denounce mixed education as dangerous to faith and morals. . . . . The revelations made by Miss Whately on this subject are most important, and the voice of the father, speaking, as you say, from the grave, has served to convince all who wished to know the truth, that a system forced on us as a great boon was intended by its principal founder to serve as a means of shaking the convictions of our people, of spreading scepticism, and undermining the vast fabric of Catholicity in our country." (*Freeman's Journal,* 2nd October, 1869.)

upon true religion, it is equally essential that the doctrines of any other religious faith, which he conscientiously believes to be erroneous, should be carefully eliminated from all educational instruction, and more particularly from that publicly administered to the youthful part of the population. The question, then, arises between the two denominations of Christians into which the population of Ireland is divided, which is the true interpretation of their common faith?—a question which the debates of centuries have not decided, and which in Ireland still subsists in its fullest vitality, exacerbated by political party feeling. The attempt made, no doubt in a spirit of conciliation, to exclude from the code of religious morals to be inculcated in the public schools all points in regard to which the two sects differ, and to base it upon those general principles or maxims in regard to which they might be presumed to agree, could not unfortunately, from the nature of the case, succeed. Their differences, both in dogma and in discipline, are too profound and essential, and their general spirit too adverse to each other, to admit of a common recourse to what would be considered by each as a sort of religious and moral "caput mortuum," as a common test or instrument of religious and moral instruction. It must be recollected, that the Roman Catholic and Protestant Churches do not consider each other simply as religious communities differing in regard to certain specific doctrines, but *denounce* each other, and that not occasionally and incidentally, but fundamentally and permanently, as false and erroneous in doctrine and destructive to all the purposes of true religion. Nothing but a degree of lukewarmness or indifference as to their respective doctrines and practice, which certainly does not exist in Ireland, could reconcile Protestants and Roman Catholics to confide the early education of their children to a tutelage which, in regard to religion, could inspire confidence in neither.

The very fact that the apparently inoffensive condition made by the Kildare Place Society, that the Bible should be read without note or comment, was objected to by the Roman Catholic hierarchy, as rendering those schools unfit for children belonging to their flocks, at once illustrates in the most striking manner the entire impossibility of the establishment of any neutral ground of religious and moral education, on which the opposing parties could, consistently with their admitted doctrines, consent to meet.

The tendency of all education in Ireland to assume a sectarian or denominational character was, in fact, inevitable, and was strongly marked in regard to all the existing schools when the subject of a general system came to be considered.

As regards the extent to which the spread of education may have facilitated the purposes of civil government, it is to be regretted that the improvement has not been so marked as to enable us to produce any very positive proofs of its existence. The same offences now occur as when the system was originated. Disaffection, it is to be feared, is not diminished; jurors are still intimidated; judges insulted; agrarian outrages frequent; and those crimes which it was thought would be surely affected by education, still continue to be committed.

Under the vague name of Fenianism, the old spirit of Irish rebellion has raised its head, and still subsists with an organization more extensive and more difficult to deal with, and with adherents more numerous, (according to the remarkable avowal made by an Irish Lord Lieutenant,) than preceded the fearful outbreak of 1798.

If there exist at the present time fewer instances of that appalling distress which has at times distinguished this country, we can scarcely set this down to the account of improved education, when we look to the more obvious causes, in the actual removal of a great part of the pauper population by emigration, or its extermination by famine, and the somewhat better distribution of the remainder, by an improved system of holdings and the cultivation of the land in larger farms. But the effect of these rude remedies cannot be assigned any more to the moral effects of increased knowledge, than the results of amputation or actual cautery could be set down to a constitutional treatment of disease, by the application of lenitive medicines or change of climate.

Religious animosity cannot, unfortunately, be said to have decreased; and Ireland still exhibits the strange anomaly of a fertile land, under a temperate climate, whose inhabitants are numerous, and endowed with physical strength and intelligence in no common degree, ruled by a Government, in comparison with most others of the world, free and enlightened, under laws in themselves wise and humane, but nevertheless having a large part of its population worse fed, worse clothed, more miserably housed, and less industrious than perhaps that of any other country in Europe.

Far be it from our intention to deduce from this consideration the conclusion, that the efforts made to supply the people of Ireland with sufficient instruction should be abandoned or relaxed. On the contrary, we should rejoice to see them redoubled. It is a case in which, as well as in many others respecting the improvement of Ireland, we would more emphatically urge the manly exhortation:—

"Tu ne cede malis; sed contra audentior ito."

CHAPTER XI.

Public Works, County Rates, and Valuation.

In all inquiries into the condition of Ireland, and the best means of ameliorating it, the development of the resources of the country has been much dwelt on, and the interference and assistance of the Government recommended.

In England, abundant sources of industry were always at hand, requiring only additional facilities of intercourse to enable them to come into full and immediate operation, and holding out sufficient inducement for the investment of private capital.

In Ireland, on the contrary, it was requisite to foster and encourage production, the materials of which were still only latent, and private capital or enterprise insufficient to render them available.

This was more especially the case in works, such as the construction of roads or piers, which, from their nature, required to be undertaken by a number of individuals. The construction of the former, it must be observed, was provided for by the Grand Juries, and many fine lines of communication had been made by them; but there were extensive districts, more especially the mountainous parts of the country, out of the reach of all markets, where such works were very desirable, but where the Grand Juries were not willing to execute them, on account of the expense.

The necessity of assistance, therefore, had been so much felt, that grants of money or special authority for the execution of works had been obtained from Parliament. Such a course, however, was found to be troublesome, expensive, and inconvenient; and as the Legislature had admitted the propriety of affording encouragement and assistance, it was determined to constitute a body which should be empowered by the Government to make loans for such purposes. Accordingly, in the year 1831, an Act (called the Public Works Act, 1 and 2 Wm. IV., cap. 33) was passed, authorizing, partly by way of grant, partly by way of loan, the issue of public money to a limited amount in aid of works in Ireland.

Numerous public works, many of them of considerable magnitude, were undertaken by the Board formed under this Act, and the execution of them contributed to the adoption of improved modes of cultivation, and to the abandonment of the rude and primitive implements in common use. They opened to the officers of justice and the local authorities, places which had been the secure haunt and impenetrable refuge of the outlaw and the robber. They gave access to parts of the country hitherto inaccessible, but which possessed great capabilities, and which now were converted into fertile and useful districts. The improved communications brought the people into contact with a world hitherto unknown to them. Gaining new ideas, and finding new markets, they were stimulated in their efforts to increase the produce of their holdings. In short, to use the words of the Select Committee of 1830 on Irish Poor, when referring to those already executed, "the effects appear to have been—extended cultivation, improved habits of industry, a better administration of justice, the re-establishment of peace and tranquillity in disturbed districts, a domestic colonization of a population in excess in certain districts, a diminution of illicit distillation, and a very considerable increase to the revenue."

The principal other works undertaken were small fishery piers, which proved of great advantage to the coast towns where they were built. The shelter thus afforded to vessels gave facilities, which had not previously existed, for the transmission of agricultural produce, and the stimulus given to agriculture, created in the vicinity of the towns a prosperity which presented a striking contrast to the wild, uncultivated wastes by which they were in many instances surrounded.*

The power of making loans to individuals for the improvement of their properties had also been given to the Board; but the terms being disadvantageous to the borrower, few applications were made.†

Although successful to a great extent as regarded the construction of roads and piers, the Act was found insufficient for effecting one of the most important of public works, namely, arterial drainage.

Draining was the first part of the great work of agricultural improvement required in the country. A large portion of the lands available for tillage

* See Reports of Select Committee on Public Works in Ireland, 1835. Also, Annual Reports of the Commissioners of Public Works.

† In this measure " two important principles," say the Land Occupation Commissioners in their report, " were recognized by the Legislature with respect to the advances of money for the improvement of Ireland—first, that it was desirable and proper to give assistance, by way of loans, towards the agricultural improvement of the country; and second, that in cases in which the property of individuals would derive a permanent benefit from such works, it was just and proper to give power to persons having limited interests, or being under legal disability, to charge such property with the repayment of money advanced in aid of such improvements." " The soundness of the views thus taken by the Legislature," they add, " will be admitted by all those acquainted with the actual state of Ireland."

an l pasturage, including the richest and most productive soils, particularly through the central or interior parts of Ireland, were not alone in a state of entire neglect, but were unimprovable for want of arterial drainage; whilst other extensive districts, if not lying absolutely waste, were liable to inundations, and were only cultivated at a great risk.

From the large co-operation which would have been required among independent proprietors, and from the numerous conflicting interests,* there existed but little prospect of such works being undertaken by private enterprise. The Government, therefore, in the year 1843, passed an Act, (5 & 6 Vict., cap. 89.) giving facilities for the execution of these large and important works, and entrusting the superintendence of them to the Commissioners who had been created under the Act of William IV.

Many applications were made, and as the works were carried out the most favourable results developed themselves. Many farms were freed from the danger of periodical inundation; large dis-

* The two following cases are instances of the number of interests involved in such undertakings:—
In the case of the Blackwater, there were 3,851 acres of flooded and injured lands, possessed by 53 proprietors and 230 lessors and occupiers.
In the Ardee district there were 3,240 acres of flooded and injured lands, possessed by 112 proprietors and 376 lessors and occupiers. (See Second Report of Drainage Commissioners.)

tricts, hitherto unavailable for cultivation, were converted into productive and profitable land; and by opening a general vent for the water, facilities were given for field drainage.

Intimately connected with the Public Works undertaken by the Government, were those undertaken by the Grand Juries at the expense of the counties.

These bodies formed, as it were, the government of the counties, and in them was vested the power of imposing rates upon the counties for local purposes. The laws regulating the imposition of these rates are of the greatest importance: by them the means of internal communication are made and maintained; in them are involved the comfort of all classes of the community, the employment of the poor, and the execution of the Public Works—the funds being devoted to the making and maintenance of roads, to the erection of public buildings, to the support of the police, and to charitable purposes.

There existed at all times on the part of the people a want of confidence in the Grand Juries, as regarded the discharge of their fiscal duties. The county rates were leviable alone upon *occupiers;* but, as many of the Grand Jurors who were chosen from the landed proprietors, and were supposed to be representatives of the proprietary interest of the different districts, held or occupied only small portions of their own estates, they contributed little of the tax they imposed. The burthen of taxation, too, had of late considerably augmented from the increase of roads, the salaries of a greater number of officers, the building of court-houses, the police establishments, and indemnification for damages for malicious injuries. These and other heavy charges were thrown upon the occupiers, and were imposed by the Grand Jurors, "enclosed," as Judge Day remarked, "within locked doors, uninterrupted by those who pay, and who hear nothing of the burden, till those who create it are dissolved and disappear."

This was a practice in direct opposition to one of the best-established principles of taxation.

The execution of the works, moreover, was anything but satisfactory. All the roads under the control of the Grand Juries could have been both better and more economically made and managed than they were. Plans were hastily adopted without sufficient investigation, and the execution of a new line of road or of a bridge was often committed to some farmer enjoying the patronage of a Grand Juror, or if more skill was requisite, was entrusted to the care of a road-jobber. In the employment of labour also, the system followed was very objectionable. Presentment work averaged about 10d. per day; but half of the advantages which the people would have derived from such employment was annulled by the manner in which they were paid, and which is described by Mr.

Nimmo, an eminent engineer, who in a letter on the subject says:—

"It appears that the repairs of roads are carried on by a class of persons who make a trade of it as a market for the labour of their tenantry. The latter are not, properly speaking, paid for what work they do, but have the amount of the presentment allowed by their landlords, as a set off against the rent of their holdings."

Nor was there any adequate check upon expenditure, the control being placed in the hands of overseers, whose mere affidavit was sufficient in accounting for the taxes received, thus leaving opportunities for frauds which were naturally but too often committed.

The system upon which the county rates were imposed and spent was not only bad, but the manner in which they were levied was unequal and unjust. Each county in Ireland is divided into baronies; each barony into townlands. When a rate was to be levied, the Treasurer of the County issued a warrant for the levy of the sum presented upon the county. The High Constable of the Barony then applotted the sum payable by his barony upon each of the townlands in it, placing an equal sum upon each of them. The injustice of such a course is at once apparent, when the great difference in the nature of the soil is considered, and the different value of the agricultural produce or rateable property of each townland. Thus waste mountain land, worth almost nothing, had to contribute to the expenses of the county in as great a proportion as arable soils bearing magnificent crops.

One example explains more clearly than can otherwise be done the injustice of such a system.

In the barony of Orrery and Kilmore, in the County Cork, the levy upon one townland was at the rate of 9s. in the pound; in another, 1s. 9½d.; and in another, 9d.* For the correction of such an unequal division of taxation, the Ordnance Survey of Ireland had been undertaken; but the other abuses became so flagrant, and the system was seen to be so faulty, that an Act for its improvement was passed in the year 1833, (3 & 4 Wm. IV., cap. 78;) and although in the year 1836 this and all former Grand Jury Acts were repealed (by the 6th and 7th Wm. IV., cap. 116,) yet the principles of the statutes being the same, we may date the commencement of the new system from 1834.

One of the first alterations it effected was to give to the tax-payers the principal, in fact almost the entire, voice in the imposition of the taxes; for it was enacted that of the persons paying the county-rates, or "cess," a certain number (selected by ballot from a list of one hundred of the highest cess-payers of the barony) were to sit and vote

* Committee, State of Ireland, 1825, p. 554.

with a certain number of magistrates at "Road Sessions," (so called, because everything relating to the roads was determined by this body,) and to the Grand Jury was left no power to make a presentment (*i.e*, to propose a tax,) for any work which had not been approved at Road Sessions. This, therefore, limited the powers of a hitherto comparatively irresponsible body. Other important alterations were also made. The fiscal duties of the Grand Juries, which formerly were performed with closed doors, were now to be performed in open court, and to avoid the evils incident to the great haste with which, owing to their limited time, they had to go through the business brought before them, they were to be summoned in time to complete the fiscal business before the arrival of the Judges, and their proceeding to the criminal business. The High Sheriff, in nominating the Grand Jury, was compelled by this Act to put one individual upon the panel from each barony of the county, thus securing a fairer representation than there had hitherto been of the interests of the different parts of the country, and annihilating a family-compact system, which to some extent had prevailed.

Measures for the economy and superintendence of the works were also taken.

Every work was in future to be executed by contract, and a county surveyor was appointed at a fixed salary to superintend the construction and maintenance of the roads and other works. Engineers being alone qualified for this situation, the advantage was gained of having a well qualified person to perform duties hitherto done by ignorant persons, and those whose principal object had been to make as much money out of the transaction as was possible.

These alterations effected a marked improvement in the administration of the fiscal powers of the Grand Juries; by the economy effected the results were highly advantageous to the tax-payer; the highways of the country were improved, so as to be inferior to those of no other, and they continue to maintain that superiority over those of England, class to class, which attracted the attention of Arthur Young so early as 1778.

The Ordnance Survey of Ireland, to which we have alluded, had been decided on in the year 1824.* It was the first step in the plan of the valuation of Ireland, which had been resolved upon by the Government, with the design of correcting the evils attendant upon that unjust method of imposing public charges which we have described; and its object was to obtain a survey of the country sufficiently accurate to enable persons appointed as valuators, and acting under Government superintendence, to follow the surveyors, and

---

* Report of Select Committee on the Survey of Ireland.

by making a valuation, to give the means afterwards of apportioning correctly and equitably the proper amount of local taxation.

As a measure of practical government, it was one of the best that has been adopted in Ireland, and it derives increased importance from the fact of its laying the foundation for effecting the valuation of Ireland, a subject of the greatest importance, whether it be considered with a view to the framing of bargains between the occupiers and owners of land, or with a view to public assessments. Although the subject had been warmly taken up in the year 1824, and a Valuation Act had been passed in 1826, much does not appear to have been done until the year 1830 or 1831. The progress of the survey, and consequently of the valuation, was very slow. When the latter was effected, the new and more equitable system of levying a proportional instead of an equal tax upon each townland was adopted. But even still a grievance, although a much lesser one, remained, in the manner of levying the rates upon the occupiers of the townland; for the proportions between the different occupiers were applotted by persons under the direction of the Grand Jury, and many of them being unfit for their work, the results attained were far from being either accurate or equitable.

The whole system, however, was simplified by the Townland Valuation Act, (6 & 7 Wm. IV, cap.

84,)* which was passed in 1836; and by the end of March, 1844, the valuation of twenty counties had been completed, that of six was in a forward state, while five counties, (in the southern part of the country,) comprising one-fourth of Ireland were untouched.†

This valuation failed, however, to be practically useful in one most important particular : it was no guide to the actual value of the several divisions of property of which the townland was composed. And then about the year 1840, a new tax, namely the Poor Rate, was imposed upon property, and the townland valuation, which was incomplete for the collection of county rates, was totally useless for Poor Law purposes; for, besides contemplating no smaller division of land than the townland, a standard of value had been adopted which failed to indicate the value re-

---

* The principle of the townland valuation (6 & 7 Wm. IV.) was based upon the scale which is appended to the Act; and that valuation was arrived at by the valuators ascertaining the actual quality of the soil, and the nature of the sub-soil; and comparing that with what, looking to the price of the produce of the country in the neighbouring markets, they thought it ought to be ; all local circumstances, whether of advantage or disadvantage, being taken into consideration.

The general townland valuation was made, therefore, according to the scale of agricultural produce appended to the Act ; but this scale of value was considerably lower than the general price of agricultural produce.

† See Select Committee on Townland Valuation, Ireland, 1844.—Evidence.

quired by the Poor Relief Act, and much property which was liable to the Poor Rates, but not to the county rates, had been omitted in the townland valuation.

It was, therefore, necessary to make a separate Poor Law Valuation; but this, though framed on a sound principle of assessment, was not sufficiently uniform to afford a basis for the imposition of the county rates. Hence there were two distinct valuations in Ireland.

As a further step in attaining a more equitable system, an Act was passed in the year 1846, (9 & 10 Vict., cap. 110,) directing that every *tenement* which was rateable under the provisions of the Poor Relief Act should be valued separately;* and thus the injustice of an inequitable payment of rates by the occupiers of a townland was removed, and each farm or holding had imposed upon it only its own proportionate share.

In the year 1852, the subject was again brought forward, and an amended Valuation Act (15 & 16 Vict., cap. 63,) was passed, in which one uniform principle of valuation for all kinds of assessments was extended to the whole of Ireland.

Thus, in place of two valuations, one of which was constructed on a faulty principle, and the

---

* The primary ingredient in this valuation was the actual value of the land, modified by the prices at the local markets, and the actual produce derived from the lands according, to the system of agriculture which prevailed in that county.

other deficient in uniformity, was substituted a single one based upon a correct estimate of value.*

It was determined also, that the valuation should undergo an annual revision, a course both necessary and useful, where the changes in the value of property are frequent and considerable.

Under this Act the valuation of the whole of Ireland has been effected, and is now annually revised.

The measure has proved to be highly advantageous to the general community. Additional securities for the correctness of the valuation have been created, through the stronger and more numerous inducements now existing for its revision. The imposition of local taxes has been rendered equitable, and their collection has been facilitated. And there is the indirect though no small advantage of a safe criterion being furnished for any Parliamentary or municipal franchise, or other public right, in which a property qualification is an ingredient.

The necessity for a correct system of valuation had become greater as the amount of taxation in-

---

* This valuation was constructed upon the intrinsic worth and capabilities of the soil, its adaptation to different descriptions of produce, and the value of the same according to the scale of prices of agricultural produce embodied in the Act, but taking the net annual value as in the Poor Law Act for houses, mines, fisheries, buildings, &c., to which such principle of comparison could not be applied.

creased; and if the system thus established is not regarded as being absolutely correct in its calculations of the actual value of property, it must be admitted that it is uniform in its results, and *relatively* correct

CHAPTER XII.

The Poor Law.

THE question of introducing a Poor Law into Ireland, could not fail at any time to engage the attention of every one who had any interest in ameliorating the notoriously wretched condition of the peasantry and lower orders in that country; but the ever-accumulating mass of destitution, arising from the rapid increase of population, the effect of the Sub-Letting Act, the periodical partial failures of the potato crop, and other causes to which we have adverted in the course of these notes, brought the subject forward more prominently about the year 1833, than at any former time.

It was consequently considered imperatively necessary to take some steps for the establishment of a general and permanent system for the relief of the poor in Ireland, similar to that existing in England, and the subject was accordingly brought under the consideration of the Legislature.

The question, however, was one in regard to which much difference of opinion existed, and may be said even still to exist. Whatever might be thought of the efficacy of the English law, and of its success in relieving the poor without injuriously encroaching on the rights of the rich, and endangering the vital principle of all just and regular government, which guarantees security to the property of its individual subjects of whatever description it may be, it was doubted that such a law could be extended to *Ireland*, consistently with the strict observance of this fundamental condition.

Nor was it unnatural that such doubts should be entertained. It was admitted on all hands, that the condition of Ireland, in regard to its poor, differed essentially from that of England. The single fact that England had long been habituated to provide by local arrangements, founded, however, upon general laws, for the relief of its destitute inhabitants, while no such provision had ever existed in Ireland, would, it was thought, constitute in itself a serious difficulty in the application of the system to the latter country. The immense scale upon which it appeared to be necessary to exercise it, compared with what was in England sufficient, although still felt there as a heavy burden, was another weighty objection urged against its practicability.

But more than all, what was calculated to cause apprehension as to the effects of a Poor Law in Ireland, was the difficulty which had been found in England itself of adjusting the provisions of the law in such a manner as to free it, not alone from inconvenience, but from the absolute *danger* to the best interests of society, which appeared at one time to be so imminent as to occupy for many years the almost entire attention of the Legislature, and to threaten even the peace of the country. The result of the agitation of this question was, as most of our readers are no doubt well aware, the passage, after much debate and strong opposition, of the Poor Law Amendment Act of 1834, which constituted a thorough reform of the existing system—a reform, however, very distasteful to a large portion of the nation, the beneficial results of which could not be immediately perceptible, and which were consequently, by many, looked upon as being of extremely dubious accomplishment.

This was a circumstance which, no doubt, retarded the consideration of the applicability of a Poor Law to Ireland. It was thought that a system which had been fraught with evil consequences in England, and had needed reconstruction, the effect of which was not yet ascertained, could not with safety be set on foot in a country where it was to be expected that the obstacles to its successful operation would be infinitely greater.

The English Poor Law Amendment Act, however, did not fail—in spite of many objections, and notwithstanding the apprehension of its opposers—to be eminently successful in effecting its objects, and in averting those evil consequences which, without the utmost care and precaution, are sure to attend any general system of compulsory State provision for the poor. The disastrous catastrophe which so soon followed the ill-judged attempt to establish such a system in France, under the name of "Droit de travail," in 1848, which its initiators pretended, at the time, was no more than a just development of the principle of the English Poor Law, is sufficient to point out the peril of such measures when not guarded and limited by restrictions requiring great practical experience to devise, as well as the exertion of sufficient authority to enforce.

In order to understand more clearly the nature of the difficulties which opposed themselves to the introduction of a Poor Law into Ireland, it may be well to advert briefly to some of the abuses of the system in England, which the Poor Law Act of 1834 was designed to remedy.

One of them was the too lavish and unequal manner in which the fund provided by the Poor Rate was distributed among its recipients. The scale of relief obtainable by the *pauper* from the Poor Law Guardians became higher than that which could be earned by the *labourer*, furnishing the latter with an obvious motive, independent of the state of idleness in which those receiving parochial relief were allowed to live, to prefer the condition of a well-fed, well-clothed, and idle participator in the public charity, to that of a comparatively worse paid and worse fed working man.

This naturally tended to an indefinite increase of the former class, carrying with it all the demoralization attendant upon dependent idleness, as contrasted with the respectability of him who feels that he owes his livelihood to his own honest exertions. Recourse to the aid of the parish was rendered more easy by the practice of " out-door relief," by which he who established a claim to be entered on the parish books as a *pauper*, was entitled to receive at his own dwelling a rate of relief proportioned to his own wants and those of his family. But this practice, in itself an abuse, was infinitely enhanced by another engrafted upon it, which, if continued, would have rendered the amount of the Poor Rate such as would have constituted a positive confiscation of the interests of a great part of the landed proprietors of England. We allude to what was termed " the making-up of wages out of rates." According to this practice, the labourer who could show that the amount of the wages he was in receipt of, fell short of what was deemed necessary to support him, was entitled to claim out of the parish rates a supplementary sum, sufficient to bring them up to what was deemed sufficient. The inevitable tendency of this was an indefinite reduction in the rate of the wages of labour; for it became a matter of indifference to the labourer, so long as he received the sum necessary for his support, how much of it was paid to him in the shape of wages, and how much in that of parochial relief. To the tenant-farmer, on the other hand, it was an evident advantage that the rate of wages should fall to the lowest possible point, so long as he was enabled to supply the deficiency out of a fund to which the farmers had contributed but a very small part in comparison to that furnished by their landlord.

The amount of poor rates under this system had already in many parts of England equalled the whole rental of the land, and in some instances exceeded it. In other parts it was felt with alarm that the same result was impending.

It became evident, consequently, that in the introduction into Ireland of a system of relief for the poor, these evils, if not most carefully guarded against, would, from the condition of the country, be certain to manifest themselves in an infinitely greater degree.

Under such circumstances was it that the Legislature had to address itself to the task of preparing a Poor Law for Ireland.

The condition of the country previous to the application of the measure that was devised—an account of the measure itself, and the principles upon which it was based—its introduction into Ireland, and the changes it from time to time underwent, first demand our attention; and these being disposed of, we shall then consider its effects, and how far it answered the objects which it was intended to accomplish.

To describe the circumstances of the people for which the new law was intended, would be but to repeat was has already been stated in previous chapters. The only change which had taken place between the years 1825 and 1835 was, that the number of persons without employment had increased, as the transition to a system of large holdings was slowly yet steadily effected, and the superabundant pauper population were removed from the land. The number of persons in Ireland "out of work and in distress during thirty weeks of the year," was in 1835 estimated at not less than 585,000, the number of those dependent upon them at not less than 1,800,000, making a total of 2,385,000.* Agricultural wages, which varied from 6d. to 1s. a day, were only obtainable for a short time of the year; so that it was impossible for labourers thus circumstanced to provide against sickness, against want of employ-

---

* Third Report, Poor Law Inquiry Commission.

ment, against old age, or against the destitution of their families in the event of their own premature decease. Much less than all this, their earnings, in most cases, did not suffice to provide the necessaries of life, and they were obliged, not unwillingly perhaps, to have recourse to mendicancy to obtain the food requisite for their existence. Large numbers, therefore, betook themselves to wandering through the country, seeking, almost demanding, food from all who were able to give it to them. Naturally an immoral class, having been reared in idleness and vice, they carried with them moral as well as physical contamination. To use Mr. Nicholl's words in his First Report on the State of the Poor in Ireland—"A mass of filth, nakedness, and squalor is constantly moving about, entering every house, addressing itself to every eye, and soliciting from every hand."

It is not necessary to enter minutely into the lamentable effects of this mendicancy upon the people in general. It had become too common to be disgraceful; it was no longer disreputable to beg, to appear wretchedly clothed, or to be without any of the decencies of life; in fact the demoralization had become so great, as to have almost quenched in the breasts of the peasantry the wish or the hope of bettering their condition.

The burden of the support of this enormous mendicant class fell entirely upon the small farmers and tenants, who, although nearly as poor themselves, displayed the most remarkable charity, and gave as long as they had anything to give.

"I could not," said Bishop Doyle in his evidence before the Committee in 1830,* "if I were to speak till the sun went down, convey a just picture of the benevolence prevailing in the hearts and minds of the middling classes in Ireland."

But, however honourable this was to them as a people, and high and holy in itself, it led in its exercise to the greatest social evils. Given without system or without inquiry to the good and to the bad, the really destitute and the pretenders to destitution alike received their maintenance out of the earnings of the industrious. Begging was encouraged rather than otherwise, and a general improvidence evinced itself among the people from the very consciousness that the last halfpenny or the last potato would be shared with the first applicant for help.

On the most moderate computation the amount of spontaneous alms was from one to two millions sterling annually; but so far from this immense expenditure being productive of any good results, the evils of mendicancy were fast becoming so intolerable, and the class of mendicants so extended, that its suppression became at last a necessity for the welfare of the State. It is evident, however,

---

* See evidence given before the House of Commons' Committee of 1830, to inquire into the state of the poor in Ireland.

that mendicancy cannot be suppressed unless some provision is made for the destitute; and partly with this view, partly with the view of assisting the people in the great transition they were undergoing, it was determined to introduce a Poor Law into Ireland.

As was naturally to be expected, so important an innovation met with considerable opposition.

It was argued that the amount of destitution in Ireland was so great that any system for the relief of the poor must inevitably break down, and that the recognition of any legal claim for relief would infallibly lead to universal pauperism, and would amount to a total confiscation of property; and the example of England for many years was held to bear out this argument.

But on the other hand more powerful arguments were brought forward.

The population must be supported in some way out of the resources of the country; and the establishment of a system, guarded by a test of destitution, would diminish rather than increase the charge. It was but fair, too, that the burden should be borne by all classes; for, as we have seen, it had hitherto fallen on one alone—the upper classes generally, and the absentee proprietors entirely, escaping from their share. It was argued, also, that a legal provision for the poor would be for the interest of every class: of the landlord—for having to support the poor he would find it to his advantage to provide them with labour, and the capital and labour so employed would yield him an ample profit; of the farmer, as it would reduce in some degree the immoderate competition for land, and would rid him of those sturdy vagrants who preyed upon his industry; of the labourer, for it would give him a refuge should he fall into absolute want.

There were other and more general ways, too, in which it was argued that a Poor Law would be beneficial. It would improve the social relations of Ireland, and would be a promoter of concord, by showing the disposition of the State to attend to the welfare of all classes; it would tend to preserve the peace of the country, by preventing vagrancy and removing some of the incentives to crime; and it would promote a kindly feeling between the upper and lower classes of the community.

A more eloquent or clearer *resumé* of the necessity of introducing such a law into Ireland, has never been given than is contained in the concluding paragraph of Mr. Nicholl's first report to the Government on this subject, in 1836:—

"It appears then, I think," says he, "that a Poor Law is necessary for relieving the destitution to which a large portion of the population is now exposed. It appears, too, that circumstances are at present favourable for the introduction of such a measure. A Poor Law seems also to be necessary, as a first step towards bringing about improvement in the habits and social condition of the people. Without such improvement, peace, good order, and security cannot exist in Ireland; and without these it is in vain to look for that accumulation of wealth and influx of capital, which are necessary for developing its resources agricultural and commercial, and for providing profitable employment for the population. Ireland is now suffering under a circle of evils, producing and reproducing one another. Want of capital produces want of employment; want of employment, turbulence and misery; turbulence and misery, insecurity; insecurity prevents the introduction and accumulation of capital, and so on. Until this circle is broken, the evils must continue and probably increase. The first thing to be done is to give security; that will produce or invite capital; and capital will give employment. But security of person and property cannot co-exist with extensive destitution. So that, in truth, the reclamation of bogs and wastes—the establishment of fisheries and manufactures—improvements in agriculture, and in the general condition of the country—and lastly, the elevation of the great mass of the Irish people in the social scale, appear to be *all* more or less contingent upon establishing a law providing for the relief of the destitute."

It is doubtful, however, that these arguments would have prevailed had not the English Poor

Law been amended, whilst the subject of the Irish Poor Law was under consideration ; and the highly satisfactory results, consequent on the change, made evident the fact, that a measure similar to the amended English law might with safety be introduced into Ireland.

Several very important principles are embodied in a law for the relief of the poor, and several questions of the greatest difficulty are involved.

The first was that of the provision of the funds, and upon this head there was much difference of opinion.

It is evident, however, that a public duty of this sort should be performed by all classes in proportion to their means ; but more especially by those who chiefly would have the means of averting pauperism by giving employment, and by discouraging evil practices. It was decided, therefore, that the fund should be obtained by a compulsory assessment in due proportion on property ; thus compelling the wealthier classes, absentee as well as resident, to bear their part of the burden. But as it was considered that proprietors were not the only class who would have a pecuniary interest in lessening the evils of pauperism, the burden was apportioned between them and their tenants.

The funds thus raised were to be managed and distributed by a certain number of persons elected by the rate-payers. As economical an administration as possible was thus secured; for it was obvious that those who were to provide the money would not be lavish in its expenditure.

But the most difficult problem to be solved was how to obtain a test of the real destitution of the applicants for relief; for it is upon this point that the whole success of the law hinges. Hitherto there had been none—the worthy and the unworthy having alike wandered from door to door, and having been alike the recipient of alms.

In England the workhouse had been found to be a test such as was required, but it was feared that it would be less efficient in Ireland. The governing principle of the workhouse system is this : that the support which is afforded at the public charge in the workhouse, shall on the whole be less desirable than the support obtained by independent exertion. To carry out this principle, it may seem to be necessary that the inmates should be in all respects worse situated, worse clothed, worse lodged, and worse fed than the independent labourers of the district. In Ireland, therefore, it was thought that there could not be the same security, in this respect, for the efficiency of the workhouse test, which might in some degree be operative in England ; and the great objection urged against its introduction into Ireland was the fact, that the physical comforts would be greater in the workhouse than in the cabins; for in Ireland no change for the worse could be made, nor a lower scale of diet be given than that upon which they subsisted. But the plan of giving lesser comforts in the workhouse was not altogether the keystone of the system. Much of its efficacy was to be found in their internal management. The compulsory labour, the discipline, the separation, or classification which was pursued in the interior, all were real objects of dislike to the pauper, and served to render the workhouse, in those respects, little better than a prison. Hence, although the inmates were as well clothed, and generally better lodged and better fed than the agricultural labourer and his family, yet the irksomeness of the discipline, and the privation of certain enjoyments, produced such disinclination to enter them, that nothing short of destitution would induce the able-bodied labourer to seek refuge therein ; and if driven thither by necessity, he would quit it again as speedily as possible, and strive (generally with increased energy) to obtain subsistence by his own efforts.*

In Ireland, therefore, although the food and accommodation in the workhouse would, from the lower status of the Irish poor, be superior in comparison to that of England, and the Irish workhouse would thus possess greater inducements ;

* See Mr. Nicholl's first Report.

yet there were countervailing circumstances in Ireland which more than balanced this difference. The Irish are by nature less submissive to restraint than almost any other people. Naturally, or by habit, they are of a migratory nature, hopeful, sanguine, fond of change; and rather than bear the restrictions of confinement, the Irishman, if in possession of health and strength, would wander the world over to obtain a living.

Upon these principles the Irish Poor Law was based, and in the year 1838, the Act (1 and 2 Vict., cap. 56) was passed.

The task of introducing the Poor Law into Ireland was one of the greatest magnitude. "Indeed," says the Annual Register of 1838, "a more arduous and momentous experiment than that which it involved, is perhaps unknown in the annals of our legislation."

There existed hitherto but few institutions for the relief of the poor, these being houses of industry, medical charities, and lunatic asylums. There was, therefore, this advantage, that Ireland was open for the establishment of a single rule and a single system, in detail as well as in principle.

The country was divided by the Act into 130 unions, each of which, as afterwards marked out, consisted of a market-town as a centre, with the district surrounding it, and in each of which a workhouse was to be erected. The unions were further divided into what were called electoral divisions; and for the administration of the law, a Board of Guardians was appointed, constituted principally of the representatives of the electoral divisions of the union. Each such division was rated for the number of poor it sent to the workhouse—a plan which was designed for the purpose of creating a local interest in the law, and ensuring its economical administration; and the funds were to be provided by a tax, at a certain sum in the pound, on the net value of the property.* No relief was to be given to anyone except *in* the workhouse, and the Act did not confer a *right* to relief.

* For ascertaining the value of property, a new valuation had to be made, for the Poor Law Act required each tenement to be rated separately, and this had not been done under the townland valuation. A valuation was accordingly made in each union, in many cases by tenant-farmers, in others by surveyors; but from the different ways in which these valuations were carried out, and their being estimated on data varying throughout Ireland, the result was an unequal valuation. It was nevertheless adopted, and used until a fairer and more equal one was made. Upon this valuation, the rates were accordingly struck; and according to the Act, each electoral division of the union was charged the proportion incurred, in respect of persons relieved in the workhouse, who were stated in the registry to have been resident in each electoral division.

The Act defines the meaning of "annual value" to be the rent at which such property, one year with another, in its actual state, might be reasonably expected to let from year to year, on the supposition that the annual average cost of repairs, insurance, and other expenses necessary to maintain the property in its actual state, and all rates, taxes, and public charges (except tithes) are to be paid by the tenant.

Mr. Nicholls, from whose works extracts have been made in the preceding pages, and who played the most prominent part in the great task of preparing the measure, proceeded, by the direction of the Government, to Ireland with four assistant Commissioners, for the purpose of carrying the new law at once into operation.

Extremely vague and exaggerated notions were entertained of the law itself and its probable effects. By unwearied exertions, however, the Commissioners succeeded in removing the alarm and misapprehension; and before long, nearly all opposition subsided, and the law, if not universally popular, was, at least, universally acquiesced in.

Considerable difficulties were surmounted in the formation of the unions, and more especially in their division into electoral divisions; for there were some districts heavily charged with pauperism, while others were comparatively free from it; yet it was necessary that the burden should be equally divided, and rendered as little oppressive as possible.

At the end of March, 1839, 22 unions had been declared, and of March, 1840, 104. In 1840, the first workhouse was opened; and as the only mode of relief, sanctioned by the Act, was that to be given within its walls, the Poor Law only then came into operation. The building of the workhouses, though an extensive and difficult operation, progressed, however, satisfactorily. In the year 1841, the whole of Ireland was placed in unions, and in the year 1846, the last workhouse was opened.

The working of the Act thus introduced into Ireland, appeared, in those places where it was in full operation, to be satisfactory, and augured well for the ultimate success of the measure.

It was not long, however, before some changes became necessary. The pressure of distress in June, July, and August, 1842, was felt with more than ordinary severity, and in 1843, considerable opposition was made to the payment of the rates.

It was found, too, in practice that the number of small rate-payers was so large, the line of demarcation between them and the destitute so difficult to draw, and the amount to be collected from the lower class so small, when compared with the cost and trouble of collection, that it became desirable to amend the law.

Accordingly, in the year 1843, an important change was made by an Act of Parliament, (6 and 7 Vict., cap. 92,) which enacted that the occupiers of holdings of a less value than £4 per annum should be exempted from the payment of the rates, which consequently fell to the share of the landlord.

The difficulties in the collection of the rates were thus removed. But the Act had another important effect; for by rendering the landlord liable for the rates of land from which he derived little or no benefit, it gave a fresh stimulus to clearing off the pauper population, and held out a fresh inducement to him to proceed in the system of consolidating the farms on his property.

Until the autumn of 1846, when the famine came, the Poor Law had not been found inadequate to the general necessities of Ireland; but the occurrence of such an event was a contingency altogether above the powers of a Poor Law to provide for.

In the increasing distress, it became at once insufficient for the numbers that stood in need of relief. The workhouses filled immediately to inconvenience; and as no relief could be given except within them, they ceased to be a sufficient resource for destitution.

Other measures, which will be described in another place, were accordingly resorted to for alleviating the distress of the first and worst of the famine years; and while they were in operation, the question was being very hotly discussed as to extending the Irish Poor Law, and giving relief to the poor *outside* of the workhouse.

The calls upon the Imperial exchequer were urgent and repeated, and an agitation was set on foot upon the principle that the property of Ireland should support the poverty of Ireland.

Unable to withstand the pressure, the Government passed a measure (10 & 11 Vic., cap. 31) authorizing out-door relief; and thus at a time when in all cases property was reduced in value, and in some was already entirely swept away, it was settled that property should be made answerable in a much greater extent for the support of poverty.

This great change from the system of in-door to out-door relief was wrung from the Legislature by the distressing circumstances in which the country was placed by the successive failures of the potato crop; for with starvation prevailing around, it was felt that it would be impossible to restrict relief to that given within the workhouse.

The effect of such a measure would have been fatal, had not the wisdom of the Legislature to some extent averted most of its evil results.

The workhouse was still to be a test of destitution, for out-door relief was only to be given when it was full; the sick and infirm were as much as possible to be placed on the out-door lists, and room thus made in the workhouses for able-bodied paupers demanding relief.

Instances might be cited of the efficiency of this plan in checking applications; but another important check was put on the number of those qualified for relief, by the 10th section of the Act, commonly known as the Quarter-Acre Clause, which declared that—

"Occupiers of more than a quarter of an acre of land were not to be deemed destitute, nor to be relieved out of the poor-rates."

In the great crisis of the famine, thousands gave up their miserable holdings to qualify as recipients, and this single clause aided to a great extent in hurrying forward the transition from small to large holdings.*

Experience, however, soon showed that the abuses and shortcomings incidental to out-door relief could not be altogether prevented.

The scene on the occasion of its administration is vividly described by one of the witnesses before the Committee of the House of Commons on the Poor Law, in 1849.†

In the year 1848, no less than 610,463 persons received relief in, and 1,433,042 outside of the workhouse; and in the year 1849, the respective

---

* An Act (10 & 11 Vic., cap. 90) was passed also in this year, (1847,) separating the control of the relief of the Irish poor from the control of the administration for the relief of the English poor.

† On the day of distributing relief, you will see eight hundred to a thousand people standing round the place where the relief is distributed, from morning till night—women, old men, and miserable creatures seeking for this relief. They are cursing and swearing, and pushing and putting each other out of the way; in short, every sort of thing that is disgusting is going on, arising from the habit of idleness, and idle talking, and intercourse, and there is every dissatisfaction that can be produced. And then their misery is very great; they are cold, they are naked, and they are dying of starvation; they have no idea of anything in the world but to get that small allowance at the instant, and they do everything that can be done to procure it if possible. (County Galway, Rev. P. Daly, 7187.)

numbers were 932,284 and 1,210,482, being considerably over 2,000,000 in each year.

As a result of the great calls made on the Poor Law, consequent on this appalling distress, the rates had risen enormously, and many of the unions became deeply embarrassed. These increased rates, too, were heaviest in those districts which were least able to bear them, weighing down many who, without this last burden, might have stood their ground—alarming all by the unaccustomed pressure of an undefined taxation, and greatly reducing the small amount of capital applicable to the employment of labour.

The sums which were remitted by legislative enactment from England during the three preceding years, amounting altogether to little short of £10,000,000, were so great as to excite alarm, which appears to have given rise to a determination on the part of the Legislature to make the property of Ireland as much as possible answerable for the relief of Irish poverty. The calamity brought on by the famine had been emphatically designated as one common to the empire, and was regarded so throughout England, until the repeated failures of the potato crop caused apprehensions as to the perpetuity of the burden, and seemed to point to the necessity of compelling the Irish people to abandon the treacherous aliment, which, it was thought, they would hardly do so long as they could turn to England for help whenever it failed them. If the consequences were thrown on Ireland itself, reliance on a crop so uncertain could not, it was thought, be persisted in.

An Act (12 & 13 Vict., cap. 24) was accordingly passed, making provision for levying a general rate throughout the country in aid of the distressed unions. The resources thus placed at the disposal of the Commissioners were of the greatest use, and enabled the guardians of the unions so assisted to provide for a time the necessaries of life for a large number of recipients, who must otherwise have been without food, the money and credit of the unions having been previously quite exhausted.

By the means thus resorted to, the extended Poor Law proved sufficient for the demands made upon it during the year of the famine. The favourable harvests of the ensuing years, and the enormous and rapid emigration, reduced the number of those receiving relief, especially of those receiving out-door relief; and owing to the increase of workhouse accommodation, the much safer system of in-door relief was re-adopted as much as possible. In the year 1853, Mr. Nicholls writes:—

"The Poor Law has nearly regained its ordinary state, after passing through the dangers and difficulties of a most calamitous visitation, and has risen from its trials with an increase of reputation, and also, it may be added, with a greatly increased capacity for effecting its objects."

In the working of the Law, however, a defect became apparent. Both the unions and the electoral divisions were too large. To remedy this, an Act (12 & 13 Vict., cap. 104) was passed in 1849, adding 32 new unions, making in all 163, and raising the number of electoral divisions from 2,049 to 3,404. By this change, a greater degree of responsibility was laid upon the individual proprietors of estates, and they could now prevent destitution on their own lands, by giving employment to their poor, without being exposed to the failure of their efforts by its existence on the adjoining properties, when they were comprised in the larger electoral divisions.

Such, then, is an account of the principal alterations effected in the Poor Law, from its introduction into Ireland down to the present time; but before proceeding to consider its effects, we must turn for a moment to two correlative subjects— the system of medical charities, and a provision for the lunatic poor.

The former had for a long time been under the consideration of the Legislature; but owing to various causes, no steps of importance had been taken. In 1851, however, a Bill was passed (14 & 15 Vict., cap. 68) which brought the rating powers and machinery of the Poor Law in aid of the medical charities. The Boards of Guardians were empowered to divide unions into dispensary districts, having regard to extent and population;

to appoint a dispensary committee; to provide necessary buildings, and such medicines and appliances as might be required for the relief of the poor; and a medical officer was to be appointed. By this Act a partial and imperfect system of medical relief, unattended with responsibility in its agents, and resting on a financial basis at once uncertain in duration, and unequal in its pressure as a tax, was exchanged for a system uniform and universal, supported out of the poor-rates, and influenced in its administration by well-defined responsibilities, under the direction and control of a central authority.* The relief given was most effectual, and great benefits were derived from the measure.

The provision for the lunatic poor, for a considerable time, was wholly inadequate as well as miserably defective. With the exception of Swift's Hospital, which cannot properly be called an asylum for the poor, one asylum, the Richmond, which had been established in Dublin, shortly after 1810, and another in Cork, with the provision of a certain number of cells in some of the county infirmaries, were the only public means taken for the relief of lunatics. Wandering lunatics, accordingly, were dispersed all over the country, going about in the most disgusting and

* See First Report of the Medical Charity Commissioners, and Annual Reports of Poor Law Commissioners.

wretched state.* To remedy this evil, authority was given to the Government, by law, to fix certain districts within which lunatic asylums should be erected, and according to which the charges for the maintenance of these establishments were to be defrayed by Grand Jury presentments. Under the Acts cited below,† several lunatic asylums were, from time to time, built, and there are now twenty-three in full working order, containing 6,200 inmates. Every place, therefore, is now provided with receptacles for their lunatic poor; so that in reference to one of the most painful afflictions to which humanity is exposed, there has been provided a system of relief as extensive as can be wished, and as perfect and effective as can be found in any other country.‡

* "There was," says a witness, examined before the Committee on Lunatic Poor, in 1817, " nothing so shocking as madness in the cabin of the peasant, where the man is labouring in the fields for his bread, and the care of the woman of the house is scarcely sufficient for her attendance on her children. When a strong young man gets the complaint, the only way they have to manage is by making a hole in the floor of the cabin, not high enough for a person to stand up in, with a crib over it to prevent his getting up. The hole is about four feet deep, and they give this wretched being his food there, and there he generally dies. Of all human calamities," concludes the witness, "I know of none equal to this in the country parts of Ireland I am acquainted with."

† 59 Geo. III., cap. 106, and 1 Geo. IV., cap. 98. Both repealed by 2 Geo. IV., cap. 33; amended by 6 Geo. IV., cap. 54, and 6 Geo. IV., cap. 14.

‡ See Annual Reports of the Inspectors of Lunatic Asylums in Ireland.

We must now revert to the consideration of the Poor Law; but to be able to measure the degree of its success, it is necessary first to state what were the results which might fairly be expected of it.

Supposing it to be the duty of a State to make some provision for its *destitute* subjects, this can never be considered as implying an obligation to support all those who may be designated, or consider themselves to belong to the classes usually designated, the *poor*. Independent of other considerations, the impossibility of providing such support is obvious; nevertheless an expectation has arisen among many, that a Poor Law would put an end to poverty. This is, of course, a misapprehension. All that it can be expected to effect is to relieve the absolutely destitute, and to keep them in sound health, until they may be able to earn their own livelihood. Other benefits, such as the diminution of mendicancy, and economy in the administration of relief, may also reasonably be expected.

According to the return of the Poor Law Commissioners, the amount expended in relief in 1868, was £707,556. There is, unfortunately, no way of ascertaining the expenditure in charity to the poor previous to the introduction of the Poor Law; but, as we have said before, the amount was estimated at from one to two millions sterling, and fell, almost with the certainty of a tax, upon one class alone. The burden is now, however, borne by all classes; so that besides being considerably less in amount, it is more equitably distributed. Thus one good effect has followed the introduction of the law.

One of the chief criterions of the success of any system of Poor Law, is to be found in the degree which mendicancy has been diminished in consequence of its operation. A fund for the relief of the destitute having been provided by a tax, is calculated in itself to reduce their number; for the tax-payer would no longer be inclined to give in alms what he had already been compelled to pay in the shape of a Poor Rate; consequently, without the enactment of any penalties, the practice of mendicancy would tend to disappear. But for many years it was lamentably apparent that no such satisfactory result was arrived at, and it was not until the year 1847, that any serious diminution took place.

After that period it rapidly declined—a reduction in which famine and emigration played a very important part—the result being that mendicancy appeared from a concurrence of these causes to have been almost entirely abandoned.

To those who were more immediately the subjects of the operation of this law, it has been indeed an assistance—relieving hundreds of thousands each year in their distress.* It has been of the greatest use in helping them through the hardships entailed upon them by the transition from small holdings to large ; it has improved the condition of the population, by inducing the great

* *Aggregate Number Relieved continuously and successively during the Years* 1840-1869.

Year.	In-door.	Out-door.	Total.	Expense.
				£
1840	10,910	...	10,910	37,057
1841	31,108	...	31,108	110,278
1842	87,604	...	87,604	281,233
1843	87,898	...	87,898	244,374
1844	105,358	...	105,358	271,334
1845	114,205	...	114,205	316,025
1846	243,933	...	243,933	435,001
1847	417,139	...	417,139	803,684
1848	610,463	1,433,042	2,043,505	1,835,634
1849	932,284	1,210,482	2,142,766	2,177,651
1850	805,702	368,565	1,174,267	1,430,108
1851	707,443	47,914	755,357	1,141,647
1852	504,864	14,911	519,775	883.267
1853	396,436	13,232	409,668	785,718
1854	310,608	9,008	319,616	760,152
1855	269,794	35,432	305,226	685,259
1856	212,579	4,557	217,136	576,390
1857	186,235	4,588	190,823	498,889
1858	177,205	5,851	183,056	457,178
1859	153,706	5,425	159,131	413,712
1860	170,549	8,965	179,514	454,531
1861	203,422	14,008	217,430	516,769
1862	267,807	23,342	291,149	578,789
1863	288,713	28,911	317,624	605,981
1864	264,569	31,266	295,835	596,465
1865	252,606	36,390	288,966	600,549
1866	232,556	37,617	270,173	611,891
1867	258,650	58,696	317,346	676,776
1868	289,471	50,257	339,728	707,556

landed proprietors of Ireland, whether resident or absentee, to look more closely after their properties, and to give employment to the poor.

In addition to these highly satisfactory results, there were other incidental advantages. To sum these up we may quote the evidence of a gentleman who for fifteen years had been the chairman of an union.*

" It has," says he, " brought the higher, the middle, the lower classes together; it has removed a great many of their prejudices ; it has supplied the upper classes with a great deal of additional local information which it was impossible for them to have a knowledge of, except through the middle classes. The middle classes have had their minds enlarged by daily contact with the *ex officio* guardians ; and the interest which is taken in the poor by the two classes has made the poor look up to them with a great deal more affection than they had for them before. . . . I believe there never has been a law which produced the same amount of good."

* T. V. Stewart, Esq., Chairman of Letterkenny Union— Committee on Poor Relief, 1861.

CHAPTER XIII.

Municipal Corporations.

Many years did not elapse after the passing of the Roman Catholic Emancipation Act, before another subject, to some extent connected with that measure, pressed itself upon public notice.

This was the state of municipal corporations in Ireland.

When emancipation was granted, the general principle was accepted that Roman Catholics were, in all cases, to be regarded as possessing equal rights with their Protestant fellow-subjects. But the Act, having no effect upon municipal corporations, the equality, so far as concerned them, did not take place; and it was with the view of effecting it, as well as of correcting other abuses in them, that a demand was raised for their reform. The social changes, too, which had taken place, the greater diffusion of wealth, and other circumstances, demonstrated that the corporations were no longer suited to the altered condition of the country nor supplied its wants.

The municipal institutions in England and Scotland had, in the year 1835, undergone considerable alterations, and had been the subject of no little debate ; but in Ireland the question was more difficult, complicated, as it was, with religious and political differences which did not affect the other parts of the empire.

The existing municipal corporations in Ireland were not indigenous to the country. They were of English importation, and when first introduced were mere outworks and defences for maintaining English authority amid a rude and hostile people.

The first charter was granted by Henry II. in 1172 or 1173, "to the men of Bristol of his city of Dublin, to inherit and hold of him and his heirs all liberties and free customs which the men of Bristol had at Bristol through all his territory ;" and several other towns were, from time to time, incorporated as circumstances demanded, the object being always the protection of the English and of English trade.

In the reign of James I. numerous charters were granted with the exclusive object of giving support to Protestant interests. A new Parliament was assembled in Ireland in the year 1613, after an interval of several years, during which no

Parliament had sat, and during which seventeen new counties had been formed, and forty new boroughs had been created. The creation of these boroughs appears plainly to have been designed to increase in the new Parliament the influence of the Crown; for those who had acquired large possessions from its bounty, became the heads and free burgesses of the new corporations, and representatives of the new boroughs. The boroughs were, in fact, exclusively Protestant, sending into Parliament a large body of new members, whose presence King James required to control the party then adverse to him, and possessing considerable power in the Irish House of Commons, and they continued, until the Union, to be the property of those on whose estates they were situated, a circumstance which was practically acknowledged by their being made the subjects of pecuniary compensation when they were abolished.*

The English inhabitants of Irish towns thus erected by Royal charter or grant into a commonalty or corporation, acquired the privileges of having a town council of their own, of making laws for their own government, and of appointing magistrates for the administration of the same. Thus those events, which we have described in a previous chapter (Chap. V.) as affecting the system

* Of the ninety-five Corporations existing in Ireland at the time of the Union, eighty were governed by charter of a date subsequent to James I.

of the Government of the country and the administration of justice, produced also an effect on the Irish corporate bodies; and the Revolution of 1688, which excluded the Roman Catholics from all share or voice in the State Government, completed their exclusion also from all participation in the corporations.

These bodies, therefore, became exclusively Protestant; and they maintained in the towns that Protestant ascendancy which had become a necessity to the existence of the integrity of the empire. For a century after this date no important change seems to have taken place.

In the year 1793, when what has been termed the Emancipation Act of the Irish Parliament was passed, corporate rights were conferred upon the Roman Catholics. The benefit, however, they derived was only nominal; their long exclusion from the exercise of this right having, in general, deprived them of the chief claims to it, and their Protestant fellow-citizens being little disposed to extend to them the municipal freedom by special grant.

Thus it was that the Emancipation Act of 1829 failed to have any real effect upon the constitution of Municipal Boroughs in Ireland, and that the question required to be separately dealt with.

The term Municipality may be considered to mean an incorporation of persons connected with a particular district, enabling them to conduct its local civil government. Accordingly, the administration of justice in domestic tribunals, the preservation of the public peace within it, by a magistracy chosen by the corporate body, and the imposition of tolls to be employed for local purposes, were the principal objects of these institutions.

The exclusion of the Roman Catholics was not, however, the only limitation which the Irish corporations underwent.

Select or governing bodies became established within them, which exercised the privilege of deciding on claims for admission. It followed, accordingly, that in many towns there was no recognised commonalty, whilst in others it was entirely disproportioned to the number of inhabitants, and was of an exclusive character, comprising neither the mercantile interest, nor representing the wealth or intelligence of the municipality. The members were frequently relatives and adherents of particular individuals, and their acts had rarely any connection with the common benefit of the district, or the wishes of its inhabitants.*

The Corporations were not, therefore, without reason looked upon by the great body of the inhabitants of the corporate districts with suspicion and distrust.

* See evidence before Committee on Municipal Corporations, 1835. Parliamentary Papers, 1835, vol. 27.

Since the changes had taken place, which had enabled Roman Catholics to share in the general diffusion of wealth and in the benefits of unrestricted industry, they had risen and multiplied in the middle and upper classes, so that in many of the cities they constituted not only a majority of the population, but a large proportion of the more opulent orders.

Their exclusion from the Corporations, however, was not so much a matter of complaint as their exclusion from the administration of justice; for in places where the great mass of the population was Roman Catholic, the municipal magistracy belonged entirely to the other religious persuasion, and the dispensation of local justice and the selection of juries were committed to the members of one creed exclusively.

The unpopular character of these bodies was thus aggravated by sectarian feelings; and they were considered to be calculated to keep alive those dissensions which it was now the policy of the Government to allay. In the majority of instances they were of little or no service to the community, in some injurious, in all inadequate to the objects of such institutions.

In the year 1835, a Committee of the House of Commons was appointed to examine into the state of Municipal Corporations in Ireland, and from their report it appears that there were at that time sixty Corporations in full vigour, and eleven almost extinct.

The population in corporate towns was 900,000; but such had been the effect of the exclusive practices, that the number of corporators did not exceed 13,000; of these, 8,000 were to be found in four boroughs; so that there were only 5,000 corporators distributed among the remaining boroughs, and regulating the affairs of a population considerably over 500,000.

The greatest abuses, moreover, existed in these bodies; lavish expenditure produced but little benefit; property intrusted to them for public use was misapplied to private purposes; situations were filled by persons devoid of proper qualifications; the emoluments of office were increased to an unwarrantable degree; and large pensions were bestowed for almost nominal services.

The Corporations had almost an exclusive voice in the administration of justice within their districts. They appointed the Sheriff, whose duty it was to select the panel of jurors. In the larger towns they appointed a Recorder, whose jurisdiction was the same as that of the Assistant-Barristers in Quarter Sessions; they appointed, also, Justices of the Peace.

The necessity of a change was very generally recognised, but great diversity of opinion existed as to what that change should be. To correct the defective system of self-election, by adopting the principle of popular election, which would place the administration of justice in the hands of the dominant party, would have entailed worse results than those of the system which it was designed to correct. Such a course would have been a complete transfer of power from one party to another. When it was proposed, the greatest fears were expressed that the measure would be destructive to Protestant interests; whilst it was predicted that such institutions would be but " normal schools for teaching the science of agitation ; and the graduates in those schools, and the professors of that science, the chosen instruments to wield the civil force and dispense the public justice."

The scheme first brought forward was rejected; and for four sessions the subject attracted the attention of the Legislature. It is unnecessary here to refer to the various amendments that were proposed. It was not until the year 1840 that an Act (3 & 4 Vict., cap. 108) was passed which settled this long-debated question.

The main interest had centered in what related to the administration of justice—one party striving to obtain exclusive control, the other seeking to retain at least a share in the administration of the laws. The measure which was ultimately adopted transferred to the Lord Lieutenant of Ireland the functions hitherto performed by the corporations in this respect, and a practice similar to that pursued in the counties was adopted in the towns. The appointment of the Sheriffs, of the Recorders, and of the Magistrates was confided to powers more impartial than local and conflicting parties ever could be; and the appointment of the principal officers of the Corporations was placed beyond the arena of party strife. The superintendence of the police had already, in the majority of instances, been removed from the control of the Corporations, by the Constabulary Act of 1836; so that the reforms now made put an end completely to all participation by the municipal corporations in the executive Government of the country. The result, no doubt, disappointed those who anticipated an acquisition of power by the change; and it was this fact which led the great champion of Irish rights to state that—

"The Irish Corporation Reform Act has produced a mongrel species of corporations more dead than alive—powerless and paralyzed."*

There were, however, various objects of local administration in which considerable improvements were effected. The arrangements essential for the health and cleanliness of the communities, lighting, paving, and supplying the town with water, and the providing of funds for these purposes, were revised.

In all but ten towns, namely, Dublin, Belfast, Clonmel, Cork, Drogheda, Galway, Limerick, Lon-

* See "Ireland and the Irish," by Daniel O'Connell.

donderry, Sligo, and Waterford, the existing Corporations were abolished; and in these ten towns a franchise was vested in every burgess occupying a house rated at £10 a-year, for the election of a new municipal body. The other towns being much smaller than those above-named, so high a qualification would have rendered the number of voters very limited; so the franchise was fixed at the occupation of a house rated at £5 a-year.

The principles of popular election thus adopted, threw open the corporate offices to the body of the inhabitants of each town.

As a natural result, many of the new bodies became almost exclusively Roman Catholic; but the principal subject of strife between the two parties having been removed from the control of either, the result was not looked upon with that jealousy or distrust which must otherwise have been felt.

The measure, as a whole, has proved undoubtedly beneficial. It has tended to the more impartial administration of justice, and to the removal of suspicion, and it was in conformity with the policy of Roman Catholic Emancipation.

For now, almost thirty years, the new system has been, with slight modifications, in force; and the results have been so satisfactory, that similar provisions have been extended, by the Towns' Improvement Act, (10 & 11 Vic., cap. 34, passed in

1847; and 17 & 18 Vic., cap. 103, passed in 1854,) to smaller towns with like benefit.

At times, it is true, these bodies, more especially the older Corporations, have endeavoured to take part in party struggles; but having no longer any real political weight, such attempts have not proved seriously mischievous ; and the Corporations have betaken themselves to the fulfilment of the proper functions of such bodies.

CHAPTER XIV.

THE FAMINE.

THERE is in the cotemporary history of Ireland no event of greater importance than the famine.

Poor and insufficient as was the nature and quantity of food of the peasantry in 1825, the condition of the great mass of the people, in this respect, had suffered a still further deterioration. Whatever effect the Sub-Letting Act may have had in checking the increase of population, it had, nevertheless, considerably augmented; and by the year 1845, it was estimated at 8,300,000; and whatever improvement may have taken place in agricultural processes in some parts of the country, the disproportion between the yield of the crops of potatoes and the number of mouths to be fed, was ever on the increase. All the evils incident upon a potato-fed population were enhanced. Even the cultivation of the better description of food was given up, and that of an inferior kind substituted. The "apple" potatoes and the "cups," were found to yield smaller crops than the "lumpers," and were abandoned for the latter, which was of a soft, watery quality; unwholesome and unpalatable; more liable to failure, and more difficult to keep.

In the years 1843 and 1844, the state of the country was not alone unsatisfactory, but dangerous. Numerous riots for food occurred, and the crimes which are indicative of want and poverty increased; the lower orders were agitated, and the higher unusually alarmed.

Nor did things improve in the early part of the ensuing year. A large portion of land was in the hands of men unable to fulfil the duties of property; many of them were absentees; there was no middle class, either agricultural or commercial, and there was an enormous population on the brink of absolute starvation.

The potato crop of the year 1845 was, however, unusually large, and the early part of it was of good quality.* But about November, it was discovered that the potatoes were affected with a hitherto unknown description of disease, and it was found that not alone was a large quantity of those in the ground unfit for consumption, but that those already dug and stored, were rotting in

---

* The early crop consists of about one-sixth of the whole.

the pits. A great proportion of the crop was destroyed; but the whole amount of it having been above the average, the effects of the loss were not so severe as they otherwise would have been. Distress, nevertheless, manifested itself among the poorer classes, but did not extend to the small farmers who, owing to the success of their other crops, were able to tide over the partial loss they sustained.

But a more fearful crisis was at hand.

In the summer of 1846, the potatoes looked remarkably well, and there appeared to be every prospect of an abundant yield. Suddenly, however, at the end of July, almost in one night, a mysterious blight fell upon the plant; the leaves withered away; the stalks became black and shrivelled, and the potato itself became wholly unfit for food.

In every district throughout the country, this disease appeared, and in many not a single field escaped. Nearly the entire crop was lost, and upon the most favourable calculation, the food that was left would be scarcely sufficient to last until the ensuing November.

The first reports of this calamity were scarcely credited, but as fuller information was obtained, they were fully confirmed. The loss sustained was estimated at eleven millions and a quarter sterling, or three-fourths of the whole crop: whilst oats, which formed the other chief article cultivated by the small farmer, had also from other causes failed to a very great extent.* From bare statistics, however, it is impossible to form an adequate estimate of this loss.

The effects of such a failure were at once felt through the entire country, but in some districts, more intensely than in others. In the greater part of Ulster, (Donegal excepted,) the condition of the people had of late years somewhat improved, and there had been a tendency to the cultivation of better descriptions of food than the potato. In the eastern counties, too, the greater number were less dependent upon it; but the case was far different in the West and South, where the land was occupied almost entirely by the cottiers or small holders. In those parts, when it failed, nearly the whole population were left without the means of subsistence. At the end of the year, the price of food had risen to a great height, the feeble resources of the people had become exhausted, and in many places they had already parted with all their little property to obtain the means of supporting life. Beds, clothes, fishing-nets, everything went for food. Whatever live stock they possessed was killed and devoured — the very dogs disappeared. As the winter went on, their distress increased. Many lived on cabbages

---

* The loss in the oat crop was calculated to be four millions and a half sterling. See House of Lords' Committee on Consolidated Annuities.

and turnips for weeks, some not tasting food more than once in forty-eight hours. Thousands died from starvation. The survivors were like walking skeletons; the women in the cabins too weak to stand; the children crying with pain, their limbs wasted almost to the bone, their faces wan and haggard, and their appearance like old men and women. Half naked, they were exposed to all the inclemencies of an unusually severe winter—sharp frost and heavy falls of snow; long-continued rains and piercing winds following each other in succession. Impelled by the cravings of hunger, they flocked from the country into the cities, towns, and villages, hoping there to find some sustenance; the country became deserted, and the towns "like beleaguered cities; their streets crowded with gaunt wanderers, sauntering to and fro with hopeless air and hunger-struck look."

In the midst of this misery, acts of the most sublime heroism were frequent, and instances are cited of the last morsel of food being shared with utter strangers.*

* "In one small, wretched hovel, in which were huddled together, three families, I saw a young mother, whose rags were really no covering, much less a protection against the weather; but even here I found a poor blind woman crouching on the floor, and she was no relation to the inmates."—(Society of Friends—Mr. Foster's Account.)

"In another hovel, barely four feet high to the top of the walls, and hardly nine feet square, were a widow and a large family. They literally had no means of support. In addition to the family who owned the house, I saw in the corner, crouched

The spread of the famine rapidly levelled all localities to an equality of destitution, and the manner in which it affected the different classes of society is well described in the following extract from the Report of the Committee of the Society of Friends:—" Prices of food were so high, that those who were still able to maintain themselves and their families could not afford to spend any money except on food. The small shop-keepers consequently lost their trade. The business of the wholesale dealer and merchant was diminished, and the various branches of manufactures felt the want of demand; many of the work people were discharged. Few houses was repaired or built, and masons, carpenters, and other tradesmen connected with building, were left unemployed. The demand for clothes, nothwithstanding the great want of them, which was everywhere felt, decreased. Tailors, shoemakers, and other

upon her knees over the little turf fire, a very old and superannuated woman, constantly rocking to and fro, and muttering to herself. Her matted grey hair hung ruggedly over her dirty shrivelled face, adding to her wild and wretched appearance. She was hardly clothed at all, so miserable were the tatters with which she was partially covered. Immediately behind her, on a damp mud floor, a small pallet of straw was spread; this was her resting-place at night; and here she sat all day. It appeared that this sad object was no relation of the poor widow of the house, but with noble kindness she allowed her to remain here, and shared with her the last morsel. Surely it might be said of her as of the widow of old, ' She gave more than they all.'"— (Appendix—Society of Friends, West of Ireland.)

tradesmen of this class accordingly suffered; and the gentry, whose rents were not paid, and who had poor-rates added to their other incumbrances, reduced their expenses, and employed fewer servants and fewer labourers."

As the immediate attendant of famine, came fever, unusually malignant and fatal. It ravaged villages; it fell on isolated dwellings, causing havoc wherever it went; it entered the workhouse, and swept off the inmates at the weekly rate of twenty to five-and-twenty in the thousand. Dysentery, too, became very prevalent, and added to the list of deaths.

As the spring of 1847 advanced, supplies of food from abroad reached the country in large quantities, and were distributed to the people; and when the summer came the great distress was past.*

The harvest of 1847 was looked forward to with the most intense anxiety, and the potato crop was watched with the keenest interest. It proved for the most part prosperous, but the breadth of land planted with it was very small, being only about one-sixth of the usual quantity.

A great deal of distress accordingly occurred during the ensuing winter and the spring of 1848,

---

* Indian corn arrived in large quantities, and its price began to fall. In March, 1847, the price had fallen from £18 a ton to £13 or £14 a ton, and at the end of August, it sunk to £7 10s. a ton.

and the horrors of the previous year were repeated on a lesser scale.

But the people were encouraged by the partial success of the last crop, and those who were still able, made the most extraordinary efforts to put down seed for the ensuing autumn. With great exertions, sacrificing everything, and submitting in many cases to extreme privations, all those who possibly could, again prepared their ground and planted it. It was a last effort, and upon it many staked their all. May and June passed, and all went well; but at the close of July, the blight again made its appearance; and, although by no means so general as in 1846, it was far more so than in 1847.

So long a continuance of the same adverse circumstances naturally produced still greater destitution. The fearful scenes of the preceding years were repeated. Long privations rendered the people more susceptible to disease, and less able to combat with want and misery, and the winter of 1848-9 produced suffering as intense as that of 1846-7.

At this unhappy period the vital powers of the people had sunk to so low a point, that a fall in the temperature, a cold or wet day, was sufficient to extinguish them, and a few hours' delay in administering food was fatal.

On one occasion a poor woman, with four children, had obtained an order for out-door relief;

but on application to the guardians was refused, owing to some informality, and was sent back with the order for correction, Next morning the four children were found dead on the road. At the different distances to which their failing strength had allowed them to follow their mother, they had sunk and perished.

To add to all these horrors, cholera made its appearance in March, 1849, and spread rapidly throughout the country, destroying whole families, often almost entire villages. The position of affairs in the spring of 1849 is but too faithfully depicted in the following extract from the Address of the Society of Friends to the public:—

"Despair of succeeding at home is driving vast numbers of the most industrious of the middle class to transfer their energy, and a considerable amount of capital, to other countries, which offer a freer scope for exertion. The paupers are merely kept alive, either in the crowded workhouse, or in alarming numbers depending on outdoor relief; but their health is not maintained, their physical strength is weakened, their mental capacity is lowered, their moral character is degraded; they are hopeless themselves, and they offer no hope to their country, except in the prospect, so abhorrent to humanity and Christian feeling, of their gradual extinction by death. Many families are now suffering extreme distress, who three years since enjoyed the comforts and refinements of life, and administered to the necessities of those around them. Thus we have seen the flood of pauperism widening more and more, engulphing one class after another, rising higher and higher in its effects on society, until it threatens in some of the worst districts to swallow up all ranks and all classes within its fatal vortex."

Such prognostications were happily not destined to be fulfilled.

The harvest of 1849 proved to be a good one, and the crops generally sound and abundant. With its success confidence began to revive; land came into cultivation again, and emigration was already beginning to make a sensible effect.

The harvest of 1850 also was good; the Poor Rates diminished; a spirit of industry prevailed, and more employment was to be obtained.

The famine was stayed, and the great crisis was past.

Active measures were adopted by the Imperial Government to assist the people in this great emergency.

In former years, when seasons of partial distress occurred in Ireland, relief was afforded by local works of a public nature, upon which the destitute poor were employed, and where they received money wages to enable them to purchase food.

Accordingly when the first failure of the potato

occurred, in 1845, the old plan was reverted to; but as it was seen that this could not make up for a deficiency of food, measures were taken for the importation of Indian corn, which was the cheapest substitute for the potato; and £100,000 worth was purchased by the Government, and conveyed to Ireland. As a further means of mitigating the distress, committees for administering relief were appointed in different parts of the country, and subscriptions were raised.

Such measures sufficed for the occasion; but the failure of the potato crop in 1846, produced a condition of things which required efforts on a very different scale to meet.

Before the close of the Parliamentary Session of that year, intelligence of the disaster had reached the Government; but neither its extent nor its probable consequences appear to have been fully comprehended.

The power of affording relief from the Poor Law being limited to accommodation in the workhouses, it was manifest that where there was much distress, such a power could only be relied on to a very small extent, and that some other means must be provided for relieving the destitution of the people.

Government determined then, in the first place, to make fresh and enlarged provision for the employment of the poor; and a Bill (9 & 10 Vic., cap. 107) was accordingly passed, renewing the provisions for the execution of Public Works.

The other chief measure which they decided on adopting, regarded the importation of food.

The experience of the preceding year suggested certain limitations of their action in this respect; and it was determined that no orders for supplies of food would be sent by the Government to *foreign* countries; that the interference of Government would be confined to those districts of Ireland, in which, owing to the former prevalence of potato cultivation, no trade in corn for local consumption existed; and that in these districts the Government depôts would not be opened for the sale of food, so long as it could be obtained from private dealers at reasonable prices.

Relief Committees were again formed, and rules laid down for them to act by.

From the month of September, 1846, the system of Public Works was in active operation, under the control of a Board;* the description of work

---

* The arduous nature of the duties devolving on the Board, may be gathered from the following extract from the well-known work, "The Irish Crisis," by Sir C. E. Trevelyan.

"The resident gentry and rate-payers, whose duty it was to ascertain, as far as possible, the probable amount of destitution in their neighbourhood—the sum required to relieve it, and the works upon which that sum could best be expended—who had the necessary local knowledge, in almost every case, devolved these functions on the Board of Works. After that, to advance the funds, to select the labourers, to superintend the work, to everywhere adopted, being the construction of roads. Each month the number of persons seeking employment increased.* " The Board of works became the centre of a colossal organization."

A great number of officers was required to superintend the operations. There were employed at one time:—

      385 Surveyors and Engineers.
   2,832 Check Clerks.
   6,894 Overseers.
      132 General Clerks.
      491 Pay Clerks. Making in all

  10,734 persons.

These figures give some idea of the efforts made by the Board to meet the evil.

At the commencement of the system, the Relief Committees investigated all the claims of appli-

pay the people weekly, to enforce proper performance of the labour; if the farm works were interrupted, to ascertain the quantity of labour required for them; to select and draft off the proper persons to perform it; to settle the wages to be paid to them by the farmers, and see that they were paid; to furnish food, not only for all the destitute out of doors, but, in some measure, for the paupers in the workhouses, were the duties which the Government and its officers were called on to perform."

* In October 1846, the average daily number was 114,000
  In November „   „   „   „   285,000
  In December „   „   „   „   440,000
  In January, 1847,   „   „   „   570,000
  In February „   „   „   „   708,000
  In March   „   „   „   „   734,000

cants for work, admitting only those who were really destitute; but as the applicants increased, all effective control was lost, all attempts to check or reduce the numbers on the works became inefficacious, and many of the committees were finally compelled to abandon the practice.

The attraction of money wages, paid regularly from the public purse, led to a general abandonment of other descriptions of industry; labourers, cottiers, artizans, fishermen, farmers, women, children, all, whether destitute or not, sought a share of the public money.* The diversion of labour from the preparation of the land for the harvest of 1847 thus caused, threatened a continuance of the famine, if not a greater one, and a change in the mode of administering relief became imperative.

Other evils, too, had developed themselves. The large assemblages of labourers led to demoralization and dissoluteness, and to dangerous and illegal combinations, whilst exposure to the in-

* " They are now solely dependent on the wages received from the road works. The applicants for employment are so numerous that, in most instances, only one man in a family, and in some cases, one and a boy, woman and girl, can obtain it. The pay of a man is 10d., of a woman 8d., and a boy 6d. a-day; and when you consider that there may be broken days from sickness or severe weather, that the price of the lowest description of food is enormously high, and that families here average about seven individuals, it is not surprising that they can scarcely support life under their many privations."—See Appendix to the Report of the Central Relief Committee of the Society of Friends for the Relief of the famine in Ireland.

clemency of the weather, combined with bad clothing and insufficient food, rendered the fatalities very numerous.

Although the plan of relieving the distress by public works had thus many and great defects, owing to which it ultimately failed, yet it was so far successful that it furnished, in the sudden outbreak of the calamity, temporary relief to a large portion of the population, and gained time until some more suitable measures could be devised.

The system has been mainly condemned on account of the inutility of many of the works, but it must be remembered that *relief* was the primary object, *utility* only a secondary consideration.

The new system determined on as a substitute was embodied in the Temporary Relief Act, (10 Vict., cap. 7,) passed on the 26th of February, 1847.

Experience had shown that where relief was given in a direct form upon the principle of the Poor Law, it had generally been effective, and a similar plan was now adopted.

Food was to be given gratuitously without any labour-test of destitution being demanded, and as the expenses were to be paid by the rate-payers, it was thought that there would be a sufficient check on undue expenditure. The only test applied to applicants for relief was personal attendance (exceptions being made in favour of the sick and impotent.) The food that was given, however, was cooked.

This latter device was found to be very efficacious. Undressed food could have been sold, but being cooked, it had no value in the market except for the actual consumers, who, when they could obtain it for nothing, would not be likely to pay for it.

To carry the Act into effect, Relief Committees were formed to collect the rates, and to receive the donations of the Government, and private subscriptions. With the money thus obtained, they purchased food, formed depôts of meal and corn, erected mills and ovens, established soup kitchens, and delivered rations to the famishing population. They had, in fact, to take the place of corn-factors, millers, bakers, and provision dealers; for such had hitherto been the social condition of the people, more especially in the western parts, that there was no need of such trades, each family providing for its own wants from the land they held—no necessity for a provision trade, because all subsisted on the potato.

The Act having come into force in March, (1847,) the persons employed on the public works were gradually discharged, and the people were thus set free to follow the necessary agricultural labour.

As the spring progressed, the number of the destitute increased. In the month of April the average daily number was 2,253,505; and on the 3rd of July (1847) it had reached the maximum, when 3,020,712 persons received rations, of whom 2,265,534 were adults, and 755,178 were children.* From that date the number declined until the administration of relief ceased altogether in September, by which time the new harvest, such as it was, was available, and the people were thrown on their own resources and the provisions of the amended Poor Law.

Thus terminated, as Sir John Burgoyne, one of the Relief Commissioners, expressed it, "the grandest attempt ever made to grapple with famine over a whole country."

The success of the plan was indisputable. The relief afforded was very effective, providing for the great mass of the really destitute, and averting, to a great extent, the necessarily fatal results of a great scarcity of food.

"The Commission closed," says Sir C. E. Trevelyan, in the work which we have already alluded to, "amidst general applause—organized armies, amounting altogether to some hundreds of thousands had been rationed before; but neither ancient nor modern history can furnish a parallel to the fact that upwards of 3,000,000 of persons were fed every day in the neighbourhood of their

---

* See Monthly Reports of the Irish Relief Commissioners, 1847.

own homes, by administrative arrangements emanating from, and controlled by one central office."*

The expense, moreover, at which all this was accomplished was very moderate, amounting only to £1,557,212.†

Whilst the Temporary Relief Act was in force, the Poor Law had been under discussion in Parliament, and, as we have already stated, the extended Poor Law Act was passed in 1847, and came into operation in the autumn.

From that time all through the winters of 1847 and 1848 the sole relief administered by the Government was through the Poor Law.

Judging, then, of the measures adopted by the Government, as a whole, and making allowances for the suddenness and greatness of the crisis which they were designed to meet, we think it must be admitted that the Legislature acted with great liberality and wisdom, and if, in some instances, they failed, this is ascribable more to the difficulties of administration, than to

---

* The Irish Crisis.

† The expense incurred by the famine, up to the close of the year 1847, amounted on the whole to £7,132,268.

Under the Public Works Act (1846),	...	£476,000
„ Labour Rate Act (1846-7),	...	4,850,000
„ „ „ (for local purposes),		130,000
„ Temporary Relief Act,	... ...	1,676,268
		£7,132,268

—See the Irish Crisis, p. 110.

any inherent defect in the nature of the remedies themselves.

The task of mitigating the distress was not, however, left to the Government alone.

A noble charity was displayed not only throughout England and the whole British empire, but in the United States of America, and even other foreign countries.*

In Ireland itself, among the resident gentry, the clergy, and the wealthier class of farmers, a charity was practised, which is above all praise. All the luxuries of life were willingly foregone; kitchens were established in private houses, from whence every day soup was distributed; the greatest self-denial was exercised, and it is impossible to over-estimate the sacrifices and privations to which all classes in Ireland cheerfully submitted, in their efforts to relieve the distress surrounding them.

We shall now endeavour to note some of the changes resulting from this painful crisis. To describe all would be impossible, for they were felt in every relation of life, in every branch of commerce, in every class of society.

At the expiration of the three years of famine and distress, the material prosperity of the country was necessarily reduced to a very low

* The subscriptions confided to the British Association and principal Relief Committes in London and Dublin amounted altogether to about £800,000.

ebb. A great diminution had taken place in all its resources. Exports, imports, manufactures, all had diminished. The consumption of those articles, which peculiarly indicate prosperity, had considerably decreased. The deposits in banks had diminished to nearly one-half, and the revenue returns exhibited a progressive decline. Landed property had fallen in value nearly one-third; its letting value had also decreased. The heavy and undefined taxation of the Poor and County Rates had ruined many, whilst it had pressed with the greatest severity upon all. Hundreds of thousands of acres of land, usually in full cultivation, now lay untilled. The fisheries were destroyed—every thing denoted the utter prostration to which the country was brought.

One of the most palpable effects, however, of the famine was the positive reduction of the population.

There is, unfortunately, no information sufficiently reliable to enable us to state the numbers of those who died of starvation, nor of those that fell victims to dysentery and cholera. Fever alone is said to have carried off 250,000. The principal cause of the reduction was emigration, which took place on a scale hitherto unknown.

Consequent on this decrease, great facilities arose for consolidating farms. The famine, in fact, had the effect of hurrying rapidly forward the transition from small holdings to large, and in the three years of its duration effected what, under ordinary circumstances, must have taken a much longer time to accomplish. A desire, too, began at this time (1849) to be felt by the farmers themselves for larger holdings, and competition ran high among them to obtain adjacent land when it became vacant. The smaller farmers also felt that there was a desperate struggle before them in the change from an exclusive dependence on the potato to a dependence upon a better and safer class of food, and they made every exertion to meet it.

Another effect of the repeated failure of the potato was, that it paved the way for the progress of the other great transition, namely, from pauper tenants to independent labourers. The destruction of the con-acre system—the introduction of the payment of money wages—and principally the great consolidation of farms, gave occasion for, and indeed rendered necessary, the creation of this class.

Several important measures such as the Incumbered Estates Act, the Landed Improvement Act—each of them requiring separate consideration—were the consequences produced by this fearful visitation; so that the changes effected by them, and by the great emigration are all directly or indirectly to be ascribed to it.

CHAPTER XV.

INCUMBERED AND LANDED ESTATES ACT.

AMONGST the many subjects which the famine forced upon the attention of the Legislature, may be numbered that of the embarrassed condition of the proprietors of land in Ireland.

The habit of living considerably beyond their means, so common among the Irish gentry, had involved many of them in inextricable difficulties. Unable, in the majority of cases, to sell even a part of their property, there existed no legal impediment to their charging it with mortgages and burthens, and transmitting it with its fresh incumbrances to the next inheritor, who but too often followed the course of his predecessor; until at last, in many cases, the ostensible owner could scarcely be said to have any real property in it at all. He remained, however, in charge of it, with all the obligations of a land-owner, but without the means of fulfilling them; and thus circumstanced, was unable either to improve his property, or to encourage improvement among his tenantry.

Nor could the mortgagee interfere in the management of an estate thus circumstanced, so long as he continued to receive the interest of his loan.

Accordingly the condition of an incumbered property rapidly deteriorated. Lands nominally under cultivation were ill managed; bogs remained undrained; the waste lands unreclaimed, and, year after year, the hold of the proprietor on his estate became weaker, until, at length, it fell into Chancery, and the collection of rents devolved upon a " Receiver."

The men so-called, were appointed by the Court of Chancery to receive the rents of estates which came under its management. They were persons generally residing in town; unacquainted with the wants of an agricultural population, and having little sympathy with its pursuits.

Bad as the condition of these incumbered estates had previously been, under their management it became worse.

The Master of the Rolls himself declared in a case before him, that—

" The gross mismanagement of estates in Ireland, under Receivers in Chancery, was a matter of public notoriety, and that there were few exceptions to the general rules of mismanagement.

There being no landlord to interest himself about the land, it became divided and sub-divided into the minutest holdings, and crowded with an immense population, until, from sub-division and pauperism, the estates under Receivers became plague spots, diffusing crime and disorganization in their neighbourhoods.

In the year 1843, 1,002 estates, representing a rental of over £700,000 or one-twentieth of the nominal rental of the country, were under Receivers. In the year 1845, when the distress came, the landed gentry were called upon to make large abatements of rent, and to raise subscriptions of money for the support of the people; and in 1846, when the total failure of the potato crop took place, they were required to make still greater exertions, with more limited and fast-decreasing means. At the same time came the enormous Poor Rates and County Rates, swallowing up whatever property many of them had left, and dragging more and more into absolute ruin.

The number of estates thrown into Chancery increased accordingly to an alarming degree; and, by the year 1848, one-tenth of the rental of Ireland was under the management of the Court, some of the counties being incumbered almost to one-fourth of their entire value:* incumbrances upon many other estates, not yet under "Receivers,"

* See House of Commons' Committee on Receivers.

also increased, the annuitant ceased to receive his income, the mortgagee to receive his interest, and at last, the Legislature was obliged to adopt some measures to put an end to the critical state in which landed property was placed.

The existing laws afforded no remedy. Great impediments to the sale or transfer of land existed, arising partly from the difficulty of proving the title to possession sufficiently well to satisfy purchasers—partly from many large estates being held in limitation, the owners having only a life interest in them, and being compelled to transmit them to the next in entail.

Titles to landed property were generally in a very unsatisfactory position. The means of registration had ever been insufficient, entailing great expense in its sale or purchase, and the effect of the penal laws, which during their existence disqualified Roman Catholics from possessing it, had thrown the matter into great confusion. According to the law in force previous to 1847, it was necessary to prove sixty years of possession in order to establish a title. An expensive investigation, therefore, always took place, but its result was not binding, for the Court had not the power to secure to a purchaser an indefeasible title. Thus it was no easy matter to satisfy him that he would not be disturbed in his possession, and as a natural consequence but few purchases were made.

It was evident, therefore, that the great difficulties connected with the question could only be surmounted by bold and decisive legislation.

The difficulty as regards the title, it was thought, would be overcome by a plan which was at once novel and effective, according to which it was designed to give to a conveyance by the Court of Chancery the effect of vesting absolutely in the purchaser, discharged of all claims, the title to the land which it purported to convey to him, thus giving him an indefeasible title.

And with regard to the sale of incumbered estates, it was proposed that the person who held the first mortgage should have the power of demanding the sale of the property, which should then, irrespective of all settlements or charges on it, be put up to public auction and sold—the purchaser receiving the indefeasible Parliamentary title—and the proceeds being devoted to paying the mortgages.

It was hoped that by these plans land in Ireland would become a marketable commodity, and that it might be transferred from persons unable to derive any advantages from it, and whose possession of it retarded the prosperity of the country, to others who might be better able to discharge the duties of property, and apply capital to the improvement of the land.

The scheme was regarded at first as involving a dangerous interference with the rights of property, and doubtless much was proposed which might be inconsistent with them; but it was argued, that the interests of the community at large, as well as the interests of individuals, ought not to be disregarded for the sake of maintaining mere abstract principles, which in the existing state of society in Ireland had led to great practical injustice. It was thought that if the owners of incumbered estates were enabled to convert them into money, the balance would often be of considerable amount, and, if prudently invested, would still leave handsome incomes; and it was hoped, that by enabling them to sell some parts of their estates, they might be in a position to pay off the incumbrances on the rest. They would then be able to give their attention and capital to the improvement of what they still retained.

A measure, such as here described, was passed by Parliament in the year 1848 (11 & 12 Vic., cap. 48.) This was the First Incumbered Estates Act; but it was not found to work well, the power of applying for the sale of a property being limited to those who having a first charge upon the estate were always sure of obtaining their money, so that but very few applications were made.

In the meantime, the number of estates coming under Receivers increased, until it was estimated that on the lowest calculation estates in Ireland to the value of £1,500,000 per annum were in that condition.

An amended Act (12 & 13 Vic., cap. 77) was accordingly passed in the following year, which, besides giving enlarged powers to owners and claimants, constituted a new tribunal for the purposes of the Act.

The power for applying for the sale of the estate was extended to any incumbrancer; and it was thus made nearly impossible for the landed proprietor, who was heavily embarrassed, to maintain the mere nominal possession of an estate, which was mortgaged to its whole value.

The Commissioners appointed under the Act, commenced their sittings in October, 1849. Applications for the sale of estates at once poured in. In the first year 1,085 were received, and in the second year 801. A large quantity of land was thus all at once thrown into the market. Previous to this its value had already fallen considerably. The famine and emigration had reduced the demand, rents had been lowered, large districts were lying waste, money was scarce, and the poor-rates and county-rates were very heavy. In fact, it was stated before the Committee of the House of Commons, in the spring of 1849, that it was almost impossible to sell estates in the Master of Chancery's Office. "No one offered to buy, or they offered sums so low, that the Master would not sell."

When the Act came into operation, sales were forced, and a still greater depreciation took place. This had been foreseen; but it was hoped that it would to a certain extent be neutralized by the Parliamentary title, which conferred the great advantage of an absolute and final settlement of the rights of all parties interested in the land purchased, and gave the purchaser an interest so simple, that a deed of conveyance was almost as good as ready money.

To some extent the Parliamentary title had the effect contemplated; for it appeared that on the average, four years' additional value was obtained for land sold with it; but this was not sufficient to make up for the great loss consequent on the compulsory sale.

A great number of the heavily incumbered estates soon changed hands, many of them being broken up and divided into small or moderate sized lots; and by the year 1856, it was thought that the great mass of property requiring to be sold had been disposed of.*

* The number of petitions to the Court for the sale of estates was—

In 1850	... ...	1,085
,, 1851	... ...	801
,, 1852	... ..	503
,, 1854	... ...	414
,, 1855	... ...	362
,, 1856	... ...	273
,, 1857	... ...	226

And from August, 1857, to March, 1858, 145.
— See Incumbered Estates Commission, 1855.

By this time, not alone was frequent recourse had to the measure, but the security given to the purchaser by it was found to be so effectual, that every other sort of title had grown into disrepute. Thus the unembarrassed portion of the landed proprietors of Ireland were, through their inability to give such a title, placed at a disadvantage in the event of their wishing to dispose of their properties.

It became, therefore, an obvious injustice, that a benefit should be conferred by the Legislature upon the owner of an incumbered estate which was not extended to the unincumbered proprietor. In many instances, indeed, the latter created fictitious charges on their properties, for the purpose of enabling them to sell them through the Incumbered Estates Court, and thus give a Parliamentary title with them.

This became at last a common practice; and as there existed no reason why unincumbered estates might not also be sold with a Parliamentary title, the Legislature determined to extend to them the provisions of the Incumbered Estates Act, and accordingly, an Act (21 & 22 Vict., cap. 72) was passed in the year 1858, which, besides effecting this important extension, created a new Court called the Landed Estates Court, under the same judges and officers as the Incumbered Estates Court, and rendered its jurisdiction perpetual. Since that time no important alteration has been effected, and the Court has continued to perform the functions assigned to it.*

We may proceed, therefore, now to note the effects of these measures, and to examine how far they proved successful in meeting the emergency for which they were designed.

The first object had been the transfer of the mass of incumbered estates from the hands of embarrassed to those of solvent proprietors. This was effected in a comparatively short time, partly from the compulsory nature of the sale, partly from the advantage which the indefeasible title conferred upon the purchaser.

It must not, however, be supposed that so great a change could be made without being severely felt by some class of the community. To many people it was absolute ruin; for in the earlier years of the operation of the Act, the proceeds of

* The number of Petitions to the Court for the sale of estates was—

					Incumbered.	Uincumbered.
From 1st Nov. to 31st Dec.,	1858	.	38	2
,,	,,	,,	,,	1859	.	289	27
,,	,,	,,	,,	1860	.	327	22
,,	,,	,,	,,	1861	.	410	42
,,	,,	,, 31st Jan.,	1862	.	26	4
In the year	.	.	1863	.	456	50
,,	.	.	1864	.	429	43
,,	.	.	1865	.	432	49
,,	.	.	1866	.	404	46
,,	.	.	1867	.	401	34
,,	.	.	1868	.	343	35

Value of estates sold, £13,750,000.

the sale of the land did not suffice to meet the whole of its liabilities; and not alone was there no residue left for the owner, but those who had lent their money on mortgage—often, indeed, had invested their whole fortunes—were left unpaid.

A great extent of land passed quickly into the hands of men who were both able to manage it and who had the means of improving it. Capital became more plenty; improvements, long wanting, were now undertaken; and agriculture, to some extent, advanced.

In consequence of the facilities for the sale of large estates in small lots, a proceeding which, under the former system, was either impracticable or was attended with great expense, a great portion of the estates sold passed into the possession of a considerably larger number of persons than they had been originally owned by. In this way was brought into existence a class of purchasers that did not exist before, smaller capitalists were able to enter the market and become proprietors, and a considerable amount of local capital was applied to the improvement of the land.*

The number of small independent freeholders (a class which form a most valuable portion of the population of England) has been accordingly increased, and there has thus been diffused over the

* Of the £21,000,000 worth of land, sold between 1848 and 1859, £18,000,000 was purchased by Irishmen, and of the 7,489 purchasers, 7,180 were Irish.

soil, a number of residents more deeply interested in its effective cultivation.

In some instances these purchasers were men who intended to reside on and cultivate the land they thus acquired, and in such cases the results were beneficial. In many others, the purchases were made as a matter of speculation, and under such circumstances, the tenants did not profit by the change, for they passed from the landlord, whose family had been connected with them for generations, to men who had no sympathy with them—who lacked the old traditions of negligence combined with indulgence, and whose principal object was to get a good return for the investment. They lost also the claims which they considered they had against their landlords for the improvements which they had made upon their holdings. But in every other point of view the measure has been successful. Its second object, that of making land a marketable commodity and easily transferable, has been accomplished; and we believe that, judging of it by the effects it has produced, it must be affirmed that, both socially and materially, it has been of great benefit to Ireland.

CHAPTER XVI.

Emigration.

In any review of the condition of the people of Ireland, the subject of emigration must necessarily hold a prominent place. It is the more interesting, because it has long been the object of divergent opinions, as to its efficacy as a remedy for evils such as those under which Ireland has been labouring, and because the truth or falsehood of the conflicting doctrines held in regard to it has been now experimentally tested to a degree unequalled within modern times.

The emigration which has taken place from Ireland to the United States of America, (for that to other countries is comparatively small,) is such, it may be said without exaggeration, as the world has not witnessed since the overthrow of the Roman empire by the barbarous nations of the North, although differing from these eruptions in many essential respects. It has, in regard to its magnitude, been termed (as is familiar to our readers) the "Exodus" of the Irish nation, but the term is in every other respect inappropriate. The Irish expatriation could not have occurred in ancient times, any more than the invasion of the Goths or the expulsion of the Children of Israel from Egypt could take place in the present state of the world. The motives and effects of these migrations were altogether different. The late, and still continued, emigration from Ireland is consequently a new fact in the world's history, and one in a great measure "sui generis." Its ultimate result—whatever we may have ascertained in regard to its causes and immediate effects—cannot yet be completely known.

In order to appreciate it under the point of view in which it is the object of our treatise to regard it, namely, as being a good or an evil to the existing population of Ireland—a benefit or an injury to the empire at large—a movement to be encouraged or discountenanced by the general Government or by individuals—it will be, in the first place, necessary to determine, so far as the reliable statements which may be at our disposal will allow, what has really taken place in regard to this interesting and much debated matter.

Let the facts at our command be first stated, and then examined. We may then be able to draw, each for himself, such conclusions as they may warrant, or frankly recognize our inability to lay down any decisive doctrine where they fail.

The emigration of Irishmen of various classes to America, whether to the present United States when British Colonies, or since their independence, as well as to Canada and other British settlements, must, from the earliest times of colonization, have been considerable. Although it is not probable that any correct estimate of its amount could now be made, the numerous families of Irish name, the large number of the population obviously of Irish origin, in almost every one of the States of the American Union and of the British part of Canada, testify to the fact; but this emigration does not appear to have exceeded the limits of those which had taken place from other European countries to the New World, and must have fallen short of some of them. Spain, for example, affords, perhaps, the earliest instance of what amounted to comparative depopulation of the mother country, in consequence of the adventurous eagerness of its inhabitants to seek new settlements. No such result was ever felt, or at least ever complained of, in the earlier emigrations from Ireland, nor were they, as far as it appears, regarded as the special effects of any peculiar form or access of distress which pervaded the country, though sufficient misery, no doubt, at every time existed, partly to account for a desire of many of the population to better their condition by leaving it.

There was, however, a kind of occasional or temporary emigration from Ireland, which prevailed in later times, and still prevails to some extent, although anterior to the great movement which now principally commands our consideration.

We mean the yearly emigration, or rather migration, of Irish labourers to the agricultural districts of England and Scotland, at the season of harvest, and their return to their own country after they had assisted in reaping it. We would draw the attention of the reader to this, so to say, bastard emigration, because, although differing in kind from that which afterwards took place, it appears to have arisen in a measure from one, at least, of the same causes, viz., want of employment, and the low rate of wages in Ireland as compared to other countries.

Long before the application of steam navigation, on the decks of the small vessels, by which communication between England and Ireland was kept up, knots of these emigrants might be observed huddled together as far as the scanty accommodation of the vessels would admit, amidst cattle and pigs, and carrying little other baggage than the reaping-hook or scythe carefully swathed in hay, the instruments of their hoped-for gains. Conspicuous by their raggedness, these wanderers were easily recognised, and known under the somewhat contemptuous, but not unkindly, appellation of "spalpeens," in the English counties which they frequented. A certain degree of sympathy existed for these poor fellows, many of whom had come on foot from distant parts of Ireland, and after having crossed the channel, trudged, perhaps long, from county to county in England or Wales, giving honest labour where employment could be got, at low wages, and sustaining themselves on a quantity of food which caused the wonder and commiseration of the English peasant. They thought themselves well paid, if they could end their pilgrimage by carrying back to their hovel in Ireland, some fifteen or twenty shillings in cash, as a partial relief to the habitual poverty which reigned in these abodes. This practice continued for a long time without exciting alarm, or calling forth objection on the part of the English. On the contrary, as long as it was confined within certain bounds, it was regarded as beneficial to the agriculturist, for there are few countries, however populous or prosperous, where, at harvest times, a supply of extra hands to get it rapidly in is unwelcome; nor does the accession, if temporary and moderate in amount, involve much, if any, depreciation in the wages of labour.

But as circumstances varied, the scene was changed. The mass of Irish agricultural labour thrown into the English market rapidly increased.

Internal causes, of which we have elsewhere treated, supplied the stimulus, and steam navigation afforded the means of transporting hordes to places which had been formerly reached by a few stray individuals. Many of these did not return as formerly to their own country, when the harvest was reaped, but fixed themselves in the suburbs of towns and villages, where their presence and their habits caused them, first, to be looked upon as a nuisance, and afterwards as a subject of alarm.*

Men accustomed to subsist on the minimum of the coarsest food, to pass the nights almost without shelter, and the days in rags, had no difficulty in offering their labour at a price which would not maintain the English workman in the superior state of comfort which, to him, habit had made a necessity, and which his Poor Law practically acknowledged to be his right. The rate of wages fell; and on the other hand, as the Irish supply of labour not unfrequently exceeded the demand, masses of paupers were thrown upon the funds of the English parishes for relief—an additional burthen, which the English rate-payer was but little inclined to submit to. The complaints of this new species of foreign (as it was regarded by the English) invasion were loud, and as it was

---

* See Report of the Committee of the House of Commons to inquire into the Condition of the Irish in English cities.

really injurious to the localities which were most exposed to it, the means of preventing it were made on several occasions the subject of discussion by the public, and even by the Legislature. To check it by artificial means or legislative enactments would have been difficult, and had not circumstances turned the tide of Irish emigration violently into another and wider channel, the matter was one which must have assumed a serious aspect.

In the point from which we are now viewing Irish emigration, this transfer of Irish labourers to England had some effect in relieving Ireland of some of the pressure of its superabundant pauperism; and the large infusion of Irish which has been poured into the populations of Liverpool, Manchester, and other towns, and still subsists there, proves that the movement has not been without its permanent results.

But the causes which had been continually urging a part of the Irish population to leave their country, in the hopes of bettering their condition elsewhere, began to assume, about the years 1841 and 1842, a magnitude, and to act with an intensity, which rendered the habitual channels of emigration too narrow for the purpose. The effects of the Sub-letting Act, or rather of the policy of which it was the embodiment, and above all, the terrible visitation of the famine in 1846 and following years, at once realized to the country the fearful effects of an overwhelming population, which had far outrun the means of its subsistence, and brought into operation what political economists term its "necessary checks," but which a people are more apt to regard as the effect of the intolerable cruelty and oppression of the upper classes of society, or at best, as the inscrutable visitations of an offended Deity.

Left the alternative of dying from starvation in their own country, or of seeking elsewhere the food which their native land denied them, the struggle for escape was desperate; and as emigration offered the readiest means, it was but natural they should avail themselves of it to the greatest possible extent. The desire for emigration became universal. On the one side was a country overburdened with a population far beyond the power of employment, sunk to the lowest depths of misery, one-third of it almost wholly dependent on charity, or resorting to plunder and spoliation for the actual means of subsistence—a population cooped up within the narrow limits of an island, battling for land, the sole means of subsistence, and stopping at no crime, the perpetration of which would secure it to them. On the other side, in the far distance, were countries abounding in fertile plains, in enormous tracts of the richest soil, and rich in all the wealth which nature can bestow.

Under other conditions of the world, such an emigration as took place from Ireland, would, as we have observed, been impossible. The regions whose immense extent and inexhaustible fertility could be expected to receive and nourish such an outpouring of starving human beings, are remote, and the means of transporting it from an island to a distant continent, would have been inadequate; so that famine and disease must have been left to complete their work. But the astonishing improvements in navigation and in rail-road conveyance, which distinguish the present times, and the countless numbers of vessels of the mercantile marines of the United States and Great Britain, were at hand, and sufficed for the gigantic operation.

All those obstacles which it might be supposed would be opposed to so wholesale an emigration, appeared, in the case of the Irish, to have been smoothed away. The misery which they had for many years endured, had, to a great extent, destroyed their attachment to their native soil; the numbers of those who had already emigrated and prospered, removed the apprehension of going to a strange and untried land; while the want of means was remedied by the liberal contributions of their relations and friends who had preceded them.

Between the years 1847 and 1851, (both inclusive,) the almost incredible number of over one million Irish—men, women, and children—were conveyed in emigrant ships to America—a whole population. In 1847, 215,444 emigrated; in 1849, 218,842, and in 1851, 249,721.

Wonder was felt by Tacitus at the ever-recurring invasions of the fertile plains of Gaul, or upper Italy, by tribes of famishing barbarians, who issued from the then uncultivated wastes and forests of Germany; and he has described the phenomenon in the single well-known phrase—"Officina gentium"—(workshop for the production of nations)—applied to that country. But the marvel has now been renewed, and the inhabitant of Philadelphia or New York, as he observes ship-load after ship-load of our unfortunate countrymen thrown into his more favoured country, might well repeat the same exclamation, and feel the same surprise in regard to the inexhaustible stream of human beings, not less wretched, if less formidable, flowing from the limited territory of an island such as ours.

Until the year 1854, emigration proceeded rapidly, but from that year its progress became much slower; partly, no doubt, owing to the improved condition of Ireland, but partly, also, from the large demand for the army consequent on the Russian war. The drain, however, upon the population of Ireland thus established by emigration continues at an average of 80,000 a-year, and the population has rapidly decreased.* In 1851 it was 1,622,739 less than in 1841, and in 1861 it was 755,311 less than that of 1851.†

* 1831 to 1841 (per annum) . . 45,000.
  1841 to 1845   ,,   . . 61,242.
  1846   ,,   . . 105,955.
  1847   ,,   . . 215,444.
  1848   ,,   . . 178,159.
  1849   ,,   . . 218,842.
  1850   ,,   . . 209,054.
  1851   ,,   . . 249,721.

(The above numbers do not include those migrating to England or Scotland.)

The next include those migrating and emigrating :—

  1852   (per annum) . . 190,322.
  1853   ,,   . . 173,148.
  1854   ,,   . . 140,555.
  1855   ,,   . . 91,914.
  1856   ,,   . . 90,781.
  1857   ,,   . . 95,081.
  1858   ,,   . . 64,337.
  1859   ,,   . . 80,599.
  1860   ,,   . . 84,621.
  1861   ,,   . . 64,292.
  1862   ,,   . . 72,730.
  1863   ,,   . . 117,229.
  1864   ,,   . . 114,169.
  1865   ,,   . . 101,497.
  1866   ,,   . . 99,467.
  1867   ,,   . . 80,624.
  1868   ,,   . . 61,018.

† "Calculating," say the Census Commissioners in their Report of 1851, " the probable increase of population at the same rate as the English and Welsh population had actually increased during this decade, the population in Ireland would probably have numbered over 9,000,000 (9,018,799) instead of 6,500,000

In the discussion upon the subject of emigration, it had often been doubted whether it ever could be made the means of so sensible and permanent a diminution of the people as would to any great extent relieve the distress of those who remained at home, however beneficial it might prove to those who expatriated themselves; and the idea of giving aid to emigration by Government grants or otherwise was, on this ground, discouraged by many political philosophers and statesmen of eminence. Mr. Drummond, the author of the well-known Report of the Irish Railway Commissioners in 1836, regarded it as an "insufficient remedy for so widespread and multitudinous an evil."

The facts to which we have just adverted would seem, however, to have removed every question as to the efficacy of emigration to produce a positive and palpable lessening of the number of the inhabitants of a thickly-peopled country, and the doubt now entertained is, whether the efficacy of the remedy is not too great, and whether the poverty of the country, alleviated for a time by decrease, may not again be aggravated when that decrease shall amount to depopulation.

Other objections were offered to emigration as a means whereby the evils of over population might

(6,552,385,) and that consequently the loss of population between 1841 and 1851 may be computed at the enormous amount of nearly 2,500,000 (2,456,114)."

be remedied. It was maintained that in any emigration upon a great scale, the substantive productive power of the country would be diminished in a greater proportion than its pauper population. Those who were comparatively well-to-do, and had sufficient energy to desire to improve their condition; those who were young, strong in body, and could get together some little capital upon which to set up in a new country; those, in fine, who could pay the expense of a passage to America would, it was contemplated, depart, while the old, the maimed, the idle, and those who were in a state of hopeless poverty, would remain, and be thrown upon the country as a burden, all the more grievous from the desertion of the abler portion of their fellow-subjects.

It cannot be doubted, that in all emigration a tendency, such as has been pointed out, must exist, and it is to be believed that, in that which has taken place from Ireland, much of the population which it would have been desirable to retain in the country has been lost to it, while it is still burthened with much of that which it would have been well to get rid of; but this does not seem to have occurred in the majority of cases. The strong ties of Irish affection led to the deportation of entire families; money was sent home by those who had gone first; every species of allurement was held out, and before long, every member of the family had left the country.

A reference to the most authentic sources of information which we possess forbids us to conclude that the productive power of the country has been deteriorated, although the number of its inhabitants has indubitably been very seriously diminished.*

It might not, therefore, be unfairly presumed that emigration has been in a great measure successful in removing a part of the distress which affected the country, and, at all events, in warding off the still greater sufferings with which it was menaced at the time the voluntary expatriation of so large a portion of its inhabitants was resorted to.

It may be said, it is true, that as a cure for the evil of a population which had outgrown the means of sustenance which a notoriously ill managed and inefficient cultivation enabled its country to supply it with, emigration was but a rude remedy, carrying with it an immense amount of moral and physical suffering to a number of human beings, and resulting in a reduction of one of the greatest elements of national force and greatness, by the transfer of no unimportant part of its physical strength to other countries—to increase, perhaps, the resources of some foreign

* In 1841 there were in Ireland 13,461,300 acres of arable land, and in 1861 there was 15,464,825. The extent of land under crops has not decreased, whilst the value of live stock has risen from £19,399,850 in 1841, to £34,708,222 in 1868.

State, which might eventually be ranged in hostility against us.

It is true, that of the only two methods by which a disproportion between the number of a people and the means producible for its support can be rectified—namely, to decrease the number to be fed, or else to augment the quantity of food—the latter is of the two the preferable remedy.

But can it always be resorted to with effect? The theories of political economists of no mean standing, point out its possibility. According to these, in a country such as Ireland, possessing a good climate, an active and intelligent population, and an amount of cultivatable land sufficient to produce food for double the number of inhabitants it ever possessed,* it would only require the steady application of greater skill and industry to its cultivation, to enable it to support the redundant population.

The prospect is seductive, and the theory as an abstract proposition, perhaps not devoid of truth. It is one which, no doubt, ought to be borne in mind in every design for the improvement of Ireland; but the application of it to the circumstances of the times which now occupy our attention was clearly impossible. Such a remedy must necessarily be slow and gradual in its operation.

* See Sir Robert Kane's "Industrial Resources of Ireland."

The growth of science and the formation of habits of industry are things which an enlightened Government may, indeed, foster and encourage, but which they cannot create or command for any sudden emergency. The traditional habits and feelings of a people, generated by the events of its past history, are not to be at once reversed even by the wisest laws, or the exercise of the best conceived social policy. The Irish famine was not a blow which could be on the instant warded off or softened by better modes of culture, or a more economical distribution of farms. The good results of such measures could not be perceptible for years to come. Nay, the attempt which was already making to augment the produce of the land by the eradication of an erroneous system of tenure had, in the first instance, the effect of aggravating the very evils it was calculated to root out. The Sub-letting Act, necessary as it was admitted to be for future improvement, did little more at first than to lay bare the ulcer which was eating into the vitals of the agricultural class—an operation, it is true, indispensable for its ultimate cure.

To have recourse to emigration, or not, was no matter of choice to the Imperial Government at the time it occurred. It was, indeed, as the British and most modern Governments are now happily constituted, a matter very much out of their control. Neither the statute law of England, nor the law of opinion of the civilized world, would now allow of the forcible expulsion of a population whose presence was found inconvenient, such as was effected by Louis XIV. in regard to his Huguenot subjects; or to go further back, such as was effected by the Spaniards of the sixteenth century in regard to the Moors and Jews. Neither would any enactment be contemplated, by which the departure of any number of individuals from their country could be effectually prevented, however undesirable their expatriation might be. All that a Government could do would be, by indirect means, to encourage or discourage such a movement, as the case might be. But the means of doing so at the disposal of the British Government in either case would be clearly inadequate, if emigration was either to be impelled or to be checked upon a scale sufficient to have a sensible effect upon the numbers or the condition of the people.*

If, therefore, the statements to which we have referred can be relied on, (as no doubt they can,) we remain in the possession of two striking facts in regard to the emigration which has taken place from Ireland within the last twenty-five years :—

1st. That the population of the country has

* See Evidence given before the Committee of the House of Lords on Colonization, 1847.

been thereby diminished in number to an extent that was not generally believed to be possible ;* and

2nd. That the products of the land have not been diminished, either in quantity or in value.

It may, then, be stated as a general fact, that there are fewer mouths to be fed than before, and that there is the same, if not a greater, quantity of food with which to supply them.

If this be the case, as we assuredly believe it to be, we may congratulate the country on the success of this great though involuntary experiment. The process has not, it is true, been one free from suffering, or exempt from disadvantages, but it has effected to a great degree what was a necessary preliminary to any future amelioration. It has brought about such a reduction of the population as renders its own subsistence possible; and it has thereby, in a great measure, spared to the people of Ireland those other infinitely more terrible ordeals by which that reduction must other-

---

* Between 1841 and 1851 the population decreased about one-fifth; (19.79 persons in every 100;) from 1851 to 1861 the diminution continued, and in the decade amounted to 11.79 per cent.

In 1841 the population to the square mile was . 251
In 1851 it fell to ,, . 202
In 1861 ,, ,, . 178

thus showing a diminution between 1841 and 1861 of 73 persons to the square mile.

This diminution was directly due to emigration.

wise have inevitably been effected—famine and disease—not perhaps unaccompanied by the bloodshed, crime, and outrage, which wait upon despair.

CHAPTER XVII.

AGRICULTURE, AND LANDED IMPROVEMENT ACT.

THE peculiar systems of farming pursued in a country so entirely dependent upon agriculture as Ireland, have not been without their influence upon its condition.

From the earliest times this country seems to have attracted notice for its pastures; and until the middle of the eighteenth century continued to be an almost exclusively grazing country. About that time, however, lands hitherto in a state of commonage were enclosed, and tillage became more generally practised; but agricultural progress was retarded by the checks imposed on exportation. As these were gradually relaxed, and the means of transport facilitated, the amount of produce considerably increased, and a greater extent of land was brought under tillage. Corn, too, began to be more extensively grown; and in the year 1806, a great stimulus was given to its cultivation by a law which admitted Irish grain free of duty into England, and which thus made Ireland a participator in the advantages of the protection afforded to this important article by the English Corn Laws.

The enormous increase of the population which took place between the years 1790 and 1825, had also the effect of rendering tillage more general, the people being obliged for their support to have recourse to an exclusive use and cultivation of the potato.

Thus, at the time from which we have dated our investigation, the principal crop was the potato; corn—stimulated by English protection—being also largely cultivated.

But although tillage had become more general, and the exports of corn had increased from half a-million of quarters in 1805 to two millions of quarters in 1825, the methods of farming had made little progress. Agriculture as a science was wholly unknown; the grossest ignorance prevailed as to the commonest facts, and the implements in use were few, and of the most primitive and clumsy description.

In the northern and in some of the eastern counties, where easier access was to be had to the English markets, and where an interchange of commodities led to an interchange of ideas, some improvements were introduced; but in all other parts of the country agriculture was backward in the extreme.

In the able Digest of the evidence given before the Land Occupation Commissioners, the different systems in practice are described:—

"On holdings above one acre, and less than two to two and a-half acres, there has generally been a two years' rotation of potatoes and grain in continual succession. Up to three or four acres, a three years' rotation; and the holdings above these classes are most generally cultivated on a seven or eight years' rotation, for three or four years of which the land was 'left out to grass.'"

"Upon the whole," continues the Digest, "this principle of farming consists, first, by the application of manure to bring up the land to a certain capability of production; and then, instead of seeking to keep it either in that condition or in a progressively improving state, the effort is to take everything from it by a continued succession of the same class of exhausting crops, until it becomes incapable of returning the cost of seed and labour; after which it is left to the unaided and gradual operation of nature to recover from the effects of this destructive treatment, that it may be again exhausted, and again left for years unproductive to recover."

Thus, while small holdings precluded the possibility of a successful system of agriculture, the large holdings, except in a few parts of the country, were cultivated in a manner far from being conducive to obtaining the largest produce.

Much, doubtless, of the general apathy as regarded improvements in farming was attributable to a want of knowledge amongst the farming class, and much to their poverty.

But there were other circumstances exerting a greater influence upon them. According to the general practice prevailing at this time, the landlord built neither dwelling-house nor farm-offices, nor did he put the holding into good order before letting it to a tenant. All improvements, therefore, fell on the tenant, who either was possessed only of the capital of his own labour and that of his family, and was incapable of making them, or if he happened to be wealthier, withheld the investment both of labour and of capital, because he was not certain of being permitted to reap a remuneratory benefit from his exertions. And though, on the one hand, many cases were not shown in which the landed proprietors had taken advantage of improving tenants; and on the other it was not shown that tenants possessing long and beneficial leases of their land had brought them to a high state of improvement—

"Yet," says the Digest above referred to, " the broad and intelligible principle was not impugned, that before any man could be expected to invest wealth on his neighbour's property, he ought to have distinct security as to the way in which that wealth is to be secured to him with a reasonable profit."

It must, therefore, unhesitatingly be affirmed, that this uncertainty of receiving an adequate return for any improvements which the tenant might make upon his farm, has been one of the principal causes in retarding the development of the agricultural productive powers of Ireland; and when it is borne in mind, that the more profitable courses of cultivation were impracticable until the requisite preparatory improvements of the soil had taken place, the extent of the evil may be better realised.

Nor can it be doubted that the law of distress operated very materially in retarding improvement. This law gave an exceptional facility to the landlord for recovering the debts due to him by his tenants. Hence, but too often, he did not inquire as to the character of the person whom he received as his tenant. Competition enabled him to get a promise of a high rent, and the remedies given by law were so prompt and efficacious as to make him almost sure that he would lose nothing by the dishonesty of the tenant. The number of unfit and insolvent competitors was accordingly so great, that the solvent man, who could have improved the land, and conferred advantages upon his landlord, was beaten out of the field, being unable to compete with the high offers made by the ignorant adventurer.*

Ireland was not, however, long permitted to enjoy the advantages of protection in her corn trade with England. The principles of free trade having been more fully recognized and more generally acted on, an agitation had been set on foot for the repeal of the Corn Laws, which, it was argued, tended to keep the price always at a high rate, to the detriment of the corn-consuming classes of England. The protection given to home produce, including Irish, was considered to be injurious to the kingdom in general;† and indepen-

---

* See Address to the Statistical Society of Ireland, by Judge Longfield, in 1864.

† "The density of our population is such, that the exclusion of foreign corn has obliged us to resort to soils of less fertility than those that are under cultivation in the surrounding countries, and, in consequence, our average prices are comparatively high. The impolicy of this conduct is obvious. If we could, by laying out £1,000 on the manufacture of cottons or hardware, produce a quantity of these articles that would exchange for 500 quarters of American or Polish wheat ; and if the same sum, were it expended in cultivation in this country, would not produce more than 400 quarters, the prevention of importation occasions an obvious sacrifice of 100 out of every 500 quarters consumed in the empire, or, which is the same thing, it occasions an artificial advance of 20 per cent. in the price of corn. We do not mean to say that this statement exactly represents the amount of injury that has been inflicted by the Corn Laws, but, at all events, it clearly illustrates the principle which they embodied."—M'Culloch's Commercial Dictionary—"Corn Laws."

dently of its stimulating one branch of agriculture at the expense of another, it checked the free interchange of the goods and produce of one country with those of another. It had been found, moreover, that the removal of prohibitions had generally contributed, not only to the welfare of the consumer, but also to that of the producer. It is not necessary here to enter into an account of the agitation. The greatest opposition was made to the change, there being a natural dread on the part of the agricultural interest of the competition that must ensue on the cessation of protection.

But events, over which there was no control, necessitated the question being decided sooner than it might otherwise have been. The partial failure of the potato in 1845, and the consequent scarcity in the spring of 1846, demonstrated the evils of a restricted importation of so important an article of food; and in June, 1846, after long debates, an Act (9 and 10 Vict., cap. 22) was passed providing for the gradual reduction during the next three years of the import duty on corn, and at the end of that time, or rather on the 1st February, 1849, fixing it at the merely nominal rate of 1s. per quarter.

Before one year, however, had elapsed, there came the second and total failure of the potato crop, (in 1846,) and it was found necessary to free the trade in food from every obstruction. Accordingly, immediately on the assembling of Parliament, two other Acts were passed, (10 and 11 Vict., cap. 1 and 2,) making further reductions in the duty, and removing the restriction imposed by the Navigation Laws on the importation of corn in foreign vessels. Thus Irish grain ceased to possess that advantage in the English market which it had for forty years enjoyed.

The measure, taken as a whole, was advantageous to the empire, yet, on Ireland it inflicted a serious loss—a fact which had been foreseen and acknowledged by Sir Robert Peel in his speech on the introduction of the measure,* when he said:—

" There is one country which this measure will seriously affect, and that country is Ireland."†

The abolition of the Corn Laws exposed the agriculturists of Ireland to the competition of the rest of the world, placing the immense supplies of grain from America on a level with those of Ireland.

Other great changes in the agricultural state of the country were effected by the famine of 1846.

The surrender by the people of their holdings, consequent on poverty, emigration, or death, pushed the system of consolidation rapidly for-

* See Hansard's Parliamentary Debates, vol. 83.
† See Note, Chap. V., page 99.

ward; and when the country began to recover from the effects of the famine, tens of thousands of these small holdings had been merged into larger farms.

Instead, however, of a still greater extension of tillage taking place, the low and unremunerative price of grain, the risk of cultivating the potato, and the want of capital still prevailing, the course of agriculture tended to return to pasturage. This was a source of great irritation to the peasantry; for independently of the demand for labour being lessened, the land which had prevented them from starving was occupied by cattle, and they complained that they were ejected from their homes, and even driven from their country, to make room for the beasts of the field.

Foremost in the great work of agricultural improvement was drainage. To arterial drainage we have, in a preceding chapter, adverted; but the subject of farm drainage is as worthy of attention.

The testimony given before the Land Occupation Commissioners had, as regards this subject, established three facts.

1st. The great extent to which farm drainage was required in every district in Ireland.

2nd. The impossibility of introducing the improved and most profitable crops and modes of principles and effects of drainage on a large scale;

cultivation on wet lands until such drainage should be effected; and

3rd. The great profit attending such operations.

The truth and importance of the second consideration was soon after established by painful experience, in consequence of the repeated and almost total failures of the potato. There was no other crop that could be successfully cultivated on the lands in the state they then were, the most useful substitutes requiring the soil to be well drained.

The great want of capital in Ireland among all classes rendered it little probable that such works would be undertaken to a sufficient extent to be beneficial to the country at large. To use Sir Robert Peel's words, too, " Agricultural science in Ireland was still in its infancy." And for these reasons it was proposed that the State should advance money for the encouragement of agricultural skill and industry. A measure for this purpose, called the Landed Improvement Act, (10 Vict., cap. 32,) was accordingly passed in the year 1847.

This Act was to be carried into effect by the Commissioners of Public Works, and instructions were immediately issued by them for the information and guidance of land-owners.

Advantage was at once, and to a great extent, taken of the Act; large loans were made, and many works were commenced.

Great ignorance had hitherto existed as to the

principles and effects of drainage on a large scale; but as the increased value of drained lands was demonstrated, a considerable desire was manifested by proprietors to avail themselves of the provisions of the Act.

The progress of the works, too, was very satisfactory, and in the humid climate of Ireland, the benefits derived were even more striking than in England. The neighbouring farmer, whose land was undrained, and whose ditches were full of water, looked with wonder at the double crops of corn, and the more than double crops of turnips raised on land which the previous year exhibited the same neglect and impoverishment as his own.

In each of the years 1848 and 1849, over £350,000 was borrowed, and in the year 1850 £250,000. After that year the amount decreased; but since the Act came into operation, loans amounting to over £2,000,000 have been made, and 240,000 acres of land have been thoroughly drained.*

The most beneficial results have followed these undertakings. Much land, including some of the richest alluvial soils of the country, has been relieved from liability to injury by floods, and the crops have increased in quantity, and improved in quality.

The benefits of giving State aid being thus de-

* The average cost is stated to be £5 7s. 6d. an acre.

monstrated, the Government extended the system; and in the year 1850, an Act (13 & 14 Vict., cap. 31) was passed, which authorized loans for the erection of farm-office buildings. This assistance was necessary, to enable the proprietors of large tracts of land to fit them for letting in extensive farms to superior agriculturists This Act also was attended with considerable success.

Active exertions were made also by landlords and by private individuals with the same view.

In many parts of the country agricultural societies were formed.

The Royal Dublin Society had long taken the initiative in this respect, with very successful results; and in the year 1841 the Royal Agricultural Society of Ireland had been formed, with the object of encouraging the best systems of agriculture, of improving the breed of cattle, and of assisting local or district agricultural societies throughout the country. Prizes were given at the annual shows, and endeavours were made to stimulate the efforts of the farmers by emulation, and to spread knowledge by exhibiting the best breeds and specimens of animals, and the latest improvements in farming implements.

The efforts of the Society have been productive of the greatest good; and other similar, but smaller societies, in different parts of the country, have likewise assisted much in the general improvement of farming.

Considerable benefits were also derived from the appointment, upon some estates, of agricultural superintendents to instruct the tenantry, from improved modes of drainage, better rotations, artificial grasses, and green crops.

Valuable statistics as to the amount and nature of agricultural produce in Ireland have been prepared since the year 1847, and we are accordingly able to note the different changes which have taken place since that time. The most striking fact regards the size of the farms.

In 1841 there were 310,436 holdings, between one acre and five acres; in 1851, 88,083; in 1868, 77,108. Farms between five and fifteen acres had decreased from 252,799 in 1841, to 172,040 in 1868; whilst those between fifteen and thirty acres had increased from 79,342 in 1841, to 136,580 in 1868; and above thirty acres from 48,625 in 1841, to 158,904 in 1868.

Instructive as these facts are in exhibiting the effects of the famine and of emigration upon the farming classes, they are also interesting as showing the progress of the system of consolidation. The evils which that system was meant to remove have to a great extent ceased to exist.

Least progress seems to have been made in the amount of land under crops; but this is not to be wondered at, considering the severity with which the repeal of the Corn Laws told upon Irish agriculture.

The extent of land under crops was 5,238,575 acres in 1847, and 5,547,971 acres in 1868, including meadow and clover. But if there has not been much increase in the amount, there has been considerable change in the description of the crops making up this total.

The total acreage under cereals has decreased from 3,313,579 acres in 1847, to 2,192,979 in 1868.

Of other crops, potatoes have increased, and the cultivation of flax has been extended from 58,312 acres in 1847, to 206,483 in 1868; whilst the acreage under meadow and clover has increased from 1,138,946 in 1847, to 1,692,135 in 1869.

To obtain a general view of the crops most common in Ireland, a calculation has been made, from which it appears that in 1868, oats, potatoes, and hay occupied 79.8 acres in every hundred acres under cultivation, and that turnips occupied a larger area than wheat.

Besides all this, there were in the year 1868 9,999,393 acres in grass or pasture.

To turn now to the live stock of the country, it appears that in this respect great progress has been made. The following table shows the changes.

	Horses.	Cattle.	Sheep.	Pigs.
1841	576,115	1,863,116	2,106,189	1,412,813
1851	543,312	2,967,461	2,122,128	1,084,857
1855	576,144	3,564,400	3,602,342	1,177,605
1860	539,500	3,606,374	3,542,080	1,271,072
1865	568,142	3,497,548	3,694,356	1,305,953
1868	544,372	3,646,796	4,901,496	869,578

Calculated at the rates adopted by the Census Commissioners in 1841, the average value on holdings above one acre was £28 1s. 4d. in 1841; £47 18s. 2d. in 1851; £63 14s. 7d. in 1867; but as a great rise has taken place in the price of stock, in consequence of the improvements in the different breeds, this calculation does not represent the *real* increase. That is more appropriately shown by a calculation of Mr. Thom, who estimates the value of cattle, sheep, and pigs, in 1868 at £44,979,641; whilst the Census Commissioners in 1841 give the value of cattle, sheep, and pigs, as £14,958,270.

It thus appears that Ireland has made considerable progress in agricultural production; which, so far from having decreased in consequence of the loss of labour caused by emigration, has augmented. That it has been more remunerative is proved by the comparatively prosperous condition of the farming classes; and although each year may not exhibit such improvement as sanguine persons hope, still, when average periods are compared, a steady advance may be noted.

There is, no doubt, room for much more improvement—a vast extent of land lies still unreclaimed, much is badly drained and ill-cultivated, and requires the outlay of capital; but there is good ground for congratulation upon the progress which has already been made, and for the hope that Ireland will ere long reach a state of fair, if not eminent, agricultural prosperity.

CHAPTER XVIII.

Material Progress of Ireland—Steam Navigation—Railways, &c.

Foremost in importance among those events which promoted the material prosperity of Ireland was the application of steam to navigation.

By the years 1828 and 1829, the advantages arising from it began to make themselves felt throughout the country. In 1824, the first steamer for the conveyance of merchandise was established between Dublin and Liverpool, and its success was at once so apparent, that other steam ships soon plied across the Channel.

This rapid means of conveyance opened up the best markets for her agricultural produce, and the best, because the cheapest, market from whence to bring manufactured goods in return. It gave an increased value to many of the lesser articles of farming produce, such as eggs, poultry, and honey, which had hitherto been almost without a market, there being but little demand for such luxuries at home, and the length and difficulty of the voyage to England precluding their profitable exportation. Their transport having become not only possible, but easy, the effect was almost the creation of a new species of property, and being generally the products of the industry of the wives and children of the farmers, their sale added to the wealth of the tenants.

Facility of intercourse has tended more to a practical union between the two countries than any legislative enactments. Inland traders found their way to the English markets, labourers passed more numerously across the Channel, and people of all classes thus travelling about acquired and diffused fresh information, new ideas, and good habits, the fruits of which became more manifest as each year went by.

Another of its effects was to admit numerous small capitalists to a trade with England. Hitherto, owing to the slowness of the return in all mercantile transactions, a large capital had been required; but now the rapid transit effected so quick a return, that one-fourth of the sum sufficed to carry on the same amount of business. A great impetus was given to open up the internal communications of the country; for as the sale of agricultural produce increased, so facilities for its transmission became urgently in request. The roads were extended and improved, canals were lengthened, and steam navigation was opened on the Shannon in 1847.

The application of steam to land transit did not take place until a much later date, and it was not until the year 1834 that the first railway was opened in Ireland, nor until the year 1847 that any development of the system took place.

The results of railway communication, so strikingly exemplified in England and other countries, have not been obtained in Ireland to the extent which was expected. This want of success is mainly owing to the fact, that in the greater number of cases the traffic consists of agricultural produce alone. There are, however, symptoms that some progress has been made, a stimulus has been given to agriculture, and traffic on some of the main lines is steadily increasing.

It was expected by some, when, in 1826, all the restrictions on commerce with England were removed, that manufactures would spring up in many parts of Ireland. The long repression, however, of the few Irish manufactures which might have been carried on, had effectually destroyed them, and England had obtained such a pre-eminence in manufacturing industry, and the possession of such immense resources in skill and capital, that when Ireland was left free and unrestricted she was unable to enter into competition. The linen manufacture is the only one worthy of the name that ever existed in Ireland, and great progress has been made in it within the last forty-five years. The number of flax factories, which in 1864, was 97, had, in 1868, risen to 143, and the number of persons employed in them, at the latter date, was over 57,000. A revival is also taking place in the manufacture of worked muslins, which, at one time, formed a great source of employment to the people in the North of Ireland, and which now employs about 300,000 persons, chiefly females.

The woollen manufacture, which was once so flourishing, has, of late years, also somewhat revived; and the cotton manufacture, though small, is steadily but slowly increasing. Porter, for which Dublin is so celebrated, is now much more extensively brewed, and the exports have considerably increased.

All these circumstances have led to an increase of the wealth of the country, and to an improvement in the condition of large numbers of the people.

Speaking generally of the agricultural classes, it may be asserted, that they are now in a permanently better condition than they have been at any former period.

There have been exceptional years of greater prosperity, it is true; but the prosperity was not permanent.

The larger farmers have, in some parts of the

country, made "a great stride" to prosperity—everywhere they have made progress. More capital is invested in their farming, the quantity and quality of their stock have improved, whilst their increasing wealth is shown in the deposits in banks, the greater proportion of which are made by them, and which, since the years of the famine, have more than doubled.*

The small farmers, who are mainly dependent on tillage, do not appear to have prospered in an equal degree. Their condition has nevertheless improved, and middlemen having almost entirely passed away, they have come under the immediate control of their landlords—a change which has been highly beneficial to them. The improvement is testified by the better class of food which they consume, by their dress, and by the consumption of certain luxuries which they have not hitherto been able to afford.

The transition from small to large holdings has created a class of agricultural labourers, earning their livelihood by daily hire, and whose condition is dependent on the rate of wages.

In the year 1855, the Poor Law Commissioners instituted inquiries on this subject, and the result is thus summed up by them:—

* In 1810, there was . £5,567,851 deposited in banks.
,, 1850, ,, . 8,268,838 ,, ,,
,, 1860, ,, . 15,609,237 ,, ,,
,, 1869, ,, . 18,437,128 ,, ,,

"Universally throughout Ireland, a more continuous state of employment of agricultural labour prevails, and wages of 1s. per day are given where formerly the rate was 4d., 6d., or 8d.; while, in most parts of the country, a man's wages reach 1s. 6d., 2s., or 2s. 6d. per day at certain seasons of the year. We believe that to these facts another important element of an improved condition may be added. We allude to the greatly increased demand for the labour of females and young persons of both sexes, which materially assists in rendering the income of an average family more proportioned to their physical wants than it was formerly."

Since that date, a further increase in the rate of wages has taken place, in consequence of the continued emigration.* There is now abundant occupation to be had; indeed, in some parts of the country, there is even a want of labourers. The system of paying wages by con-acre has passed away, and money payments have been substituted.

Nor have the prices of what, to them, are the the necessaries of life increased to such a degree as to neutralize this increase in their earnings, for potatoes, which still form their diet to a considerable extent, although not so exclusively as before, have remained very cheap, whilst Indian corn has placed within their reach another article of food

* See Reports of the Poor Law Inspectors, 1870.

which is to a large extent used among them. In too many instances, however, these people are still very poor, but a great deal of their poverty is attributable to the habit of drinking, much of their earnings, which might be employed in the purchase of some of the smaller comforts of life, being thus squandered away. Still, comparing the condition of these people with that of the small farmer or cottier-tenant of some fifty years ago, the result is decidedly satisfactory, though there is still room for great improvement.

There is, perhaps, no more effectual test of the comparative prosperity of the agricultural labouring classes than the number of persons receiving Poor Law relief during the year. The relative degree of distress prevailing throughout the country is also indicated, for the distress above pauperism may be assumed to be in a constant ratio to the amount of destitution relieved by the Poor Law. We have already referred to statistics proving the diminution of destitution. A clearer view of the present amount of pauperism in Ireland is obtained by analyzing the last annual return. In the year 1868, 289,471 persons received relief in the workhouse, and 50,257 outside of it. The average daily number of able-bodied males was only 2,406, and of able-bodied females 6,133 and this out of a population of about 5,500,000.

A great improvement has also taken place in

the condition of the people as regards house accommodation.

The Census Commissioners classified the houses under four heads. The fourth class comprised all mud cabins having only one room; the third class consisted of a better description, built also of mud, but varying from two to four rooms and windows; the second were good farm-houses, or in town, houses having from five to nine rooms and windows; the first class included all houses of a better description. According to their returns, there were in

	1841	1851	1861
1st Class	40,080	50,164	55,416
2nd ,,	264,184	318,758	360,698
3rd ,,	533,297	541,712	489,668
4th ,,	491,278	135,589	89,374
Total,	1,328,839	1,046,223	995156

From this it will be seen that the number of first and second-class houses has increased. Four-fifths of the worst description of them have disappeared, and the better portion of the houses have been retained as the population diminished; and although at the time of the last census the house accommodation for the labouring classes was far from being satisfactory, yet, since then, further improvements in this respect have been effected throughout the entire country.

Thus, in these essential respects, the condition of the people has improved. Further evidence of the progress of the country is given in the increase of the imports into Ireland from foreign countries and British possessions abroad.

The value of British and Irish produce and manufactures exported direct to foreign countries from ports in Ireland has also increased; but this trade is comparatively inconsiderable. The main trade of Ireland is direct with England; and, unfortunately, no information on this subject is obtainable, as no account is kept of cross-channel traffic. One fact, however, shows its great increase, and that is the very large number of vessels which now trade between the two countries.

Another sign of improvement is, that attention is at present directed in a greater degree to the natural resources of the country. Foremost amongst these are the fisheries, both inland and coast. These do not appear to have been ever in a satisfactory condition. Large numbers of persons, it is true, followed this occupation; but, with the exception of those living at the few ports from which facilities existed for transmitting the fish to market, they do not seem to have gained any other benefit beyond earning a livelihood. Nor did they devote themselves to it exclusively, for the majority of them were in possession of small bits of land, and depended mainly on the potato.

In the crisis of the famine, these poor people became either unable to keep their nets, tackle, or boats in repair, or they were compelled to part with them for food; and, since that time, the fisheries have been in a very depressed state. Within the last few years, however, some improvement is noticeable; the demand for fish has become much greater, the transmission of it both to English and Irish markets has been facilitated, and there is reason to hope that, before long, this branch of national wealth may become fully developed.

Thus, in many important particulars, Ireland appears to have improved. There is, however, great room for further progress. Her mineral wealth, although considerable, is as yet almost untouched. She possesses many natural resources, which have not yet been fully developed; and, although it cannot reasonably be expected that she can, within any assignable period, reach that height of commercial and manufacturing wealth to which England, from a variety of concurring circumstances, has attained, yet she may reach a position little inferior, and one which will place her high in the list of the prosperous nations of the world.

CONCLUSION.

The author is conscious that the foregoing notes are calculated to convey but a summary and imperfect notion of the number and variety of the questions which must present themselves to a conscientious inquirer into the present state of Ireland. If, however, they can in any degree serve as a guide to those who may be desirous of entering upon a more complete investigation, the object he had in view in their publication will have been accomplished.

As he advanced in his inquiries he became even more fully aware of the vastness of the subject, and of his own necessary difficulties to deal with it in all its details, as well as in the due co-ordination of all its branches, and their mutual bearings upon each other as parts illustrative of the whole state of a country in a condition so anomalous and complicated, and, it is to be hoped at least, so transitory as that now existing in Ireland. He says *transitory*, for if the author has ventured to come to any general conclusion as the results of such study as he has been able to give to the subject, it is the consolatory one, that his country has made, and is still making, great progress towards prosperity.

It is true that much remains to be done. The process is necessarily slow—ardent hopes will be checked—discontent will not at once subside so soon as all just cause for it has been removed. Habits of thought and feeling, engendered by long subsisting struggles, amounting almost to the formation of a distinct national character, cannot be easily laid aside. Political convulsion will be still looked to by many as the shortest, if not the only, road to national prosperity. Outrage and defiance of the law will be mistaken for that political emancipation which it must ever retard; but the enlightened attention and dispassionate consideration which every Irish question is now sure to receive in the Imperial Parliament, combined with that firmness, tempered with indulgence, in sustaining the authority of the Government—a failure in which would now be fatal to the position and general success of any English administration—cannot but have their legitimate effect, and those who, from history's teaching, are convinced that no nation ever yet suddenly emerged from depression and sprang into prosperity will not despair.

FINIS.

www.ingramcontent.com/pod-product-compliance
Lightning Source LLC
Chambersburg PA
CBHW032354230426
43672CB00007B/694